NATIONAL CENTER FOR EDUCATION STATISTICS

Statistical Analysis Report   **March 1995**

High School and Beyond

Educational Attainment of 1980 High School Sophomores By 1992

1992 Descriptive Summary of 1980 High School Sophomores 12 Years Later

John Tuma
Sonya Geis
MPR Associates, Inc.

DISCARD

C. Dennis Carroll
Project Officer
National Center for Education Statistics

U.S. Department of Education
Office of Educational Research and Improvement   **NCES 95-304**

U.S. Department of Education
Richard W. Riley
Secretary

Office of Educational Research and Improvement
Sharon P. Robinson
Assistant Secretary

National Center for Education Statistics
Emerson J. Elliott
Commissioner

National Center for Education Statistics

"The purpose of the Center shall be to collect, and analyze, and disseminate statistics and other data related to education in the United States and in other nations."—Section 406(b) of the General Education Provisions Act, as amended (20 U.S.C. 1221e–1).

March 1995

Contact:
C. Dennis Carroll
(202) 219–1774

For sale by the U.S. Government Printing Office
Superintendent of Documents, Mail Stop: SSOP, Washington, DC 20402-9328
ISBN 0-16-045538-3

Foreword

The National Education Longitudinal Studies (NELS) program of the National Center for Education Statistics (NCES) was established to study the educational, vocational, and personal development of young people beginning with their elementary or high school years, and following them over time as they begin to take on adult roles and responsibilities. Thus far, the NELS program consists of three major studies: the National Longitudinal Study of the High School Class of 1972 (NLS-72), High School and Beyond (HS&B), and the National Education Longitudinal Study of 1988 (NELS:88).

NLS-72 followed the 1972 cohort of high school seniors through 1986, or fourteen years after most of this cohort completed high school. The HS&B survey included two cohorts: the 1980 senior class, and the 1980 sophomore class. Both cohorts were surveyed every two years through 1986, and the 1980 sophomore class was also surveyed again in 1992. NELS:88 started with the cohort of students who were in the eighth grade in 1988, and these students have been surveyed every two years since that time.

This descriptive report describes the educational attainment, employment outcomes, and family formation of the 1980 sophomore class in 1992, ten years after most of the students in that cohort graduated from high school. The report begins with an essay that explores in some detail the relationships between characteristics of the 1980 sophomores, their patterns of enrollment in postsecondary education, their postsecondary expectations, and their patterns of educational attainment in 1992. The compendium of tables that follows this essay provides summary data on the family status, employment outcomes, voting behavior, and activities of the 1980 sophomore class in 1992, as well as additional information about their educational experiences not included in the essay. Each of the four sections of the compendium is prefaced by a series of bullets that highlight the findings of the section. This format was chosen because it illustrates both the level of detail that can be achieved in an analysis that uses the HS&B Fourth Follow-up data as well as the broad scope of the information in these files.

Acknowledgements

The authors would like to thank all those who contributed to the production of this report. At MPR Associates, Laura Horn provided guidance for the project and assistance in working with the Data Analysis System. Gary Hoachlander revised the essay and smoothed out some of its rougher edges, and Andrea Livingston and Susan Choy edited the report. Lynn Sally and Karen Singson prepared the tables and graphics and provided essential production assistance, and Mark Premo was very helpful in developing the table parameter files for use with the Data Analysis System.

Paul Planchon and Jeff Owings at the National Center for Education Statistics (NCES) reviewed early drafts of the report, and offered many suggestions for its improvement. The authors would especially like to thank the members of the adjudication panel for their careful reading and thoughtful comments. Panel members from NCES were Robert Burton from the Statistical Standards and Methodology Division, Andrew Kolstad from the National Assessment of Educational Progress (NAEP) Division, and Nabeel Alsalam from the Data Development Division. Other panel members were Daniel Madzellan from the Office of Postsecondary Education in the U.S. Department of Education, and Carol Fuller from the National Institute of Independent Colleges and Universities.

Table of Contents

List of Tables

vii

List of Figures

Educational Attainment of 1980 High School Sophomores by 1992

In 1992, the National Center for Education Statistics resurveyed the 1980 high school sophomores who participated in the earlier rounds of High School and Beyond (HS&B). Ten years had passed since these students were scheduled to graduate from high school, and most were now 28 or 29 years old. This 1992 survey, the fourth followup of this cohort since the first data collection in 1980, examined many aspects of these students' early adult years—enrollment in postsecondary education, experience in the labor market, marriage and childrearing, and voting behavior, to name a few. Thus, the HS&B Fourth Followup is a rich source of information on young adults in the late 1980s and early 1990s.

For many of these young people, pursuing further education was a major activity during this stage of life, and examining patterns of enrollment and participation in postsecondary education would be of value for this reason alone. But in addition to being a major activity for many of the 1980 high school sophomores, postsecondary education was also the key to many of their subsequent transitions and achievements, including entry into the labor market, the establishment of career goals and opportunities, and family formation. Among the most important consequences of the decision to pursue a postsecondary education were the different economic outcomes stemming from it. For example, those who earned a postsecondary degree were more likely to be employed and tended to have higher earnings than did those 1980 sophomores who did not earn a postsecondary degree, and earnings generally increased along with educational attainment.[1] For all these reasons, then, it is important to understand how different decisions about postsecondary participation and enrollment are related to attainment.

The cohort's experiences and accomplishments in postsecondary education varied greatly. By 1992, two-thirds of the 1980 high school sophomores had enrolled in some form of postsecondary education. This proportion was up from 60 percent of the cohort in 1986 (the year of the third followup), indicating that some students delayed initial entry into postsecondary education until well into their mid or late twenties.[2] Of those who did enroll by 1992, 43 percent enrolled first in a 4-year institution, 37 percent in a public 2-year institution, and the remainder in some other type of postsecondary institution, most typically a private for-profit or proprietary institution. Given these general patterns of postsecondary enrollment, what levels of education did the 1980 high school sophomores attain by 1992, and how did attainment vary among different types of students? The answers to these questions have many facets. However, at least one pattern stands out. The 1980 sophomores were much more likely to earn a postsecondary credential if they enrolled in postsecondary education immediately after high school than if they delayed their entry.

---

[1]See tables in Section 3 of the table compendium following this essay for elaboration of these patterns.
[2]Data for 1986 adapted from Eva Eagle, Robert Fitzgerald, Antionette Gifford, and John Tuma, *High School and Beyond: A Descriptive Summary of 1980 High School Sophomores: Six Years Later* (Washington, DC: U.S. Department of Education, Office of Educational Research and Improvement, National Center for Education Statistics, June 1988), appendix tables C1.1 and C1.2.

This essay briefly examines the educational attainment of the 1980 high school sophomores. It not only looks at what they had accomplished approximately 10 years after high school but also describes some of the ways in which attainment varied within the cohort. Of particular interest are such issues as time of entry into postsecondary education, the relationship between attainment and postsecondary expectations at the end of high school, differences between full-time and part-time students, the amount of time taken to obtain a postsecondary credential, and the number of institutions attended during the course of postsecondary attendance. There are some interesting findings that should stimulate researchers to delve more deeply into the information provided by the HS&B Fourth Followup.

Highest Degree Attained by 1992

For many 1980 high school sophomores, the highest degree attained was not postsecondary (figure 1). As of 1992, the highest degree earned by about one-half of the cohort—including almost 36 percent of those students who had enrolled in a postsecondary institution at some time between 1982 and 1992—was a high school diploma. Moreover, by 1992, 6 percent of the 1980 sophomores still did not have a high school diploma, down from about 8 percent of the cohort in 1986.[3] Therefore, some 1980 sophomores who had not finished high school by 1986 did continue to pursue their high school studies and obtained a diploma by 1992; however, three-quarters of those who had not earned a high school diploma or its equivalent by 1986 still had not done so 6 years later. In short, by 1992, for 57 percent of those who were high school sophomores in 1980, degree attainment was limited to a high school diploma or no degree at all. While 75 percent of these students aspired to some form of postsecondary education as sophomores in high school, the majority had not completed a postsecondary credential 12 years later.[4] Indeed, one-third had not enrolled in any form of postsecondary education at all.

By 1992, 43 percent of the 1980 high school sophomores had attained some type of postsecondary credential. For 19 percent of the cohort, the highest degree attained was prebaccalaureate: 11 percent earned a vocational certificate (usually representing the equivalent of 1 full-time year of postsecondary education), and 8 percent attained an associate's degree. Twenty-four percent of the sophomores—or more than half of those earning any type of postsecondary credential—attained a bachelor's degree or higher, including 1 percent who earned a professional degree or doctorate. Given that the median time from completion of a bachelor's degree to completion of a doctorate ranged from 7.5 years in the physical sciences to more than 12 years in the humanities in 1990–91, it is not surprising that so few members of this cohort had attained a professional degree or doctorate.[5] A larger percentage of the 1980 high school sophomores should attain this status as they move into their early thirties.[6]

---

[3]Ibid., table C1.1.

[4]National Center for Education Statistics, High School & Beyond Fourth Followup Data Analysis System, 1980–1992.

[5]National Center for Education Statistics, *Digest of Education Statistics, 1993*, tables 290-95.

[6]About 3 percent of the 1980 sophomore class claimed that taking graduate or professional courses was their major activity in 1992 (table 1.3 in the Compendium).

Figure 1
Percentage of 1980 high school sophomores by highest degree attained through 1992

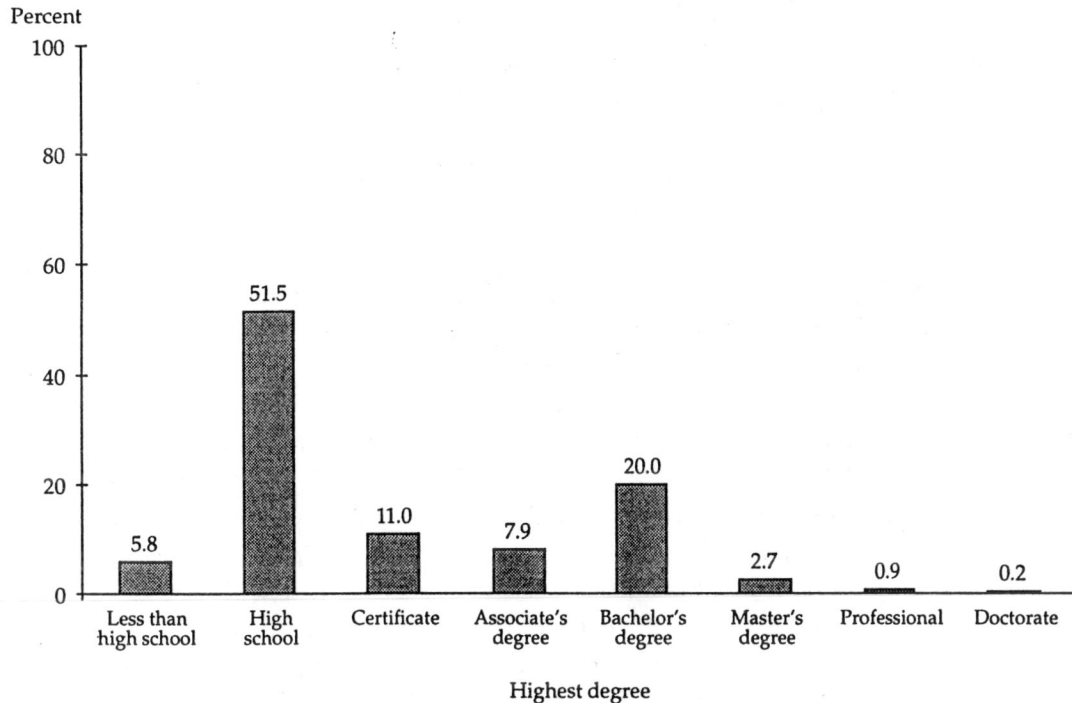

Percent

```
100 ┬
    |
 80 ┼
    |
 60 ┼              51.5
    |               ┌──┐
    |               │  │
    |               │  │
 40 ┼               │  │
    |               │  │
    |               │  │                           20.0
    |               │  │                          ┌──┐
 20 ┼               │  │            7.9           │  │
    |       5.8     │  │     11.0  ┌──┐           │  │
    |      ┌──┐     │  │    ┌──┐   │  │           │  │    2.7
    |      │  │     │  │    │  │   │  │           │  │   ┌──┐   0.9      0.2
  0 ┴──────┴──┴─────┴──┴────┴──┴───┴──┴───────────┴──┴───┴──┴──────────────────
      Less than   High    Certificate Associate's Bachelor's Master's Professional Doctorate
     high school  school              degree      degree     degree
```

Highest degree

SOURCE: National Center for Education Statistics, High School and Beyond: 1980 Sophomore Cohort, 1980–1992.

In brief, despite the emphasis in the teenage years on preparation for college, only one in four of the 1980 high school sophomores attained a bachelor's degree in the 10 years following high school. Another 20 percent or so earned some other type of postsecondary credential. For the majority of this cohort, as with the majority of students in earlier cohorts, the high school diploma was the only degree attained.

Postsecondary Attainment and Expectations as High School Seniors

Were these postsecondary outcomes consistent with the expectations of these students while in high school? In one respect, they were (table 1). Seventy-one percent of the 1980 high school sophomores who said in 1982 that they did not expect to attain any postsecondary credential attained no more than a high school diploma, and 16 percent still were not high school graduates. Of those who expected to obtain a bachelor's degree, 64 percent had earned some type of postsecondary credential by 1992. In general, postsecondary attainment rose on average with each successively higher level of educational expectations. From this perspective, therefore, the

3

postsecondary attainment of the 1980 sophomores mirrored their expectations about postsecondary education while in high school.[7]

Table 1

Percentage of 1980 high school sophomores by highest degree attained through 1992, by postsecondary expectations in 1982

Student characteristics	Highest degree through 1992							
	Less than high school graduate	High school	Certi-ficate	Assoc-iate's	Bachelor's	Master's	Profes-sional	Doctorate
Total	5.8	51.5	11.0	7.9	20.0	2.7	0.9	0.2
Postsecondary expectations in 1982								
None	15.5	71.1	9.3	3.0	1.0	0.1	0.0	0.1
Vocational-technical	4.6	61.6	19.8	10.7	3.3	0.1	0.0	0.0
Less than four-year degree	1.6	53.2	13.3	15.6	15.0	1.1	0.2	0.0
College degree	0.9	35.3	6.8	6.3	44.9	5.0	0.8	0.1
Advanced degree	0.8	28.9	5.2	5.7	45.1	9.0	4.4	0.8

NOTE: Percentages may not sum to 100 percent due to rounding.

SOURCE: National Center for Education Statistics, High School & Beyond: Sophomore Cohort 1980–1992

From another perspective, however, there was a large gap between what these young people aimed for as high school students and what they actually accomplished in postsecondary education during the ensuing 10 years. Among those who expected to achieve some level of postsecondary degree completion, less than half had actually attained their goals as of June 1992. For example, among those who in 1982 expected to complete a 4-year college degree, 51 percent had attained a bachelor's degree or higher by 1992, and this rate of attainment was typical of all students, regardless of their different levels of postsecondary expectations.[8] Thus, many students tended to

---

[7]This essay focuses on the relationship between postsecondary expectations when the 1980 high school sophomores were seniors in 1982 and their subsequent postsecondary attainment. However, for many students, postsecondary expectations were set much earlier. Data presented in tables 2.1 and 2.2 the table compendium following this essay show that students who planned to go to college while in the sixth grade were much more likely to enroll in a 4-year institution and to enroll immediately after high school than were students who planned not to go, were not sure, or had not thought about college attendance while in the sixth grade. Since it seems unlikely that students would independently reach conclusions about their eventual level of educational attainment at such a young age, these data suggest that parental encouragement from an early age has a substantial impact on the postsecondary attainment of their children.

[8]The percentage of students who had attained an advanced degree by 1992 was much smaller than half, but part of this outcome can be explained by the relatively limited amount of time that students had to achieve their educational goals.

underachieve relative to their educational expectations, and a relatively small percentage of students attained degrees that exceeded their expectations.[9]

It is possible, of course, that some of these students will still realize their postsecondary expectations at a later date. However, the preliminary evidence on this prospect, which is presented next, is not encouraging. Delaying entry into postsecondary education appears to carry with it a rather low likelihood of completion, at least during the first 10 years after high school. Barring a marked reversal in this trend, it is likely that many of the 1980 sophomores who expected to pursue postsecondary education but delayed their entry will never realize the postsecondary goals they held at the end of high school.

Postsecondary Attainment and Immediate Versus Delayed Entry

Rates of postsecondary attainment varied greatly among the 1980 high school sophomores, and one of the factors most strongly associated with these differences was the timing of entry into postsecondary education. Students who delayed their entry into postsecondary education (defined as entry after October 1982) were significantly less likely than those who entered immediately (by October 1982) to earn a bachelor's degree or higher (table 2). Forty percent of all 1980 sophomores who entered postsecondary education immediately after high school had earned a bachelor's degree by 1992, and another 7.9 percent had attained an advanced degree. By contrast, 9 percent of those who delayed entry had attained a bachelor's degree by 1992, with another 1 percent having attained an advanced degree. Overall, immediate entrants into postsecondary

Table 2
Percentage of 1980 high school sophomores by highest degree attained through 1992, by immediate versus delayed entry

| | Highest degree through 1992 | | | | |
Entry status	High school	Certi-ficate	Assoc-iate's	Bachelor's	Advanced degree
Immediate entrants	29.6	9.9	12.1	40.3	7.9
Delayed entrants	53.7	24.2	11.7	9.2	1.0

NOTE: Percentages may not sum to 100 percent due to rounding.

SOURCE: National Center for Education Statistics, High School & Beyond. Sophomore Cohort 1980–1992

---

[9]This relationship between expectations and attainment has been consistent over the last two decades at least. In his comparison of the high school classes of 1972 and 1980, Grubb concluded that expectations appear to set an upper limit to attainment and that goals are more frequently revised downward than upward. W. Norton Grubb, *Access, Achievement, Completion, and "Milling Around" in Postsecondary Vocational Education* (Berkeley, CA: MPR Associates, Inc., April 1989), 25-26.

education were much less likely to be noncompleters at the postsecondary level than were those who delayed their entry. While 30 percent of immediate entrants had still not attained any type of postsecondary degree or certificate as of June 1992, almost 54 percent of delayed entrants had not earned any type of postsecondary degree or certificate by that date.

The general patterns of differential attainment between immediate and delayed entrants persisted when educational expectations were held constant (table 3). Among those who expected in 1982 to earn some type of postsecondary degree or certificate, a larger percentage of those who delayed entry into postsecondary education than of those who entered immediately had attained only a high school degree as of 1992, regardless of the level they expected to attain. Additionally, average levels of attainment were higher among immediate than delayed entrants who had comparable postsecondary education goals.

Table 3

Percentage of 1980 high school sophomores by highest degree attained through 1992, by postsecondary expectations in 1982 among immediate versus delayed entrants

Postsecondary expectations in 1982	Highest degree through 1992				
	High school	Certi-ficate	Assoc-iate's	Bachelor's	Advanced degree
Immediate entrants					
None	49.0	29.0	15.3	6.5	0.0
Vocational-technical	39.1	29.9	23.5	7.0	0.3
Less than four-year					
degree	36.7	13.2	23.9	23.9	2.1
College degree	26.6	5.1	6.5	54.3	7.3
Advanced degree	22.3	3.5	5.4	52.0	16.7
Delayed entrants					
None	57.9	27.3	11.1	2.9	0.6
Vocational-technical	50.2	32.0	13.8	3.9	0.0
Less than four-year					
degree	57.8	18.4	12.4	10.5	0.7
College degree	54.6	15.4	8.7	19.9	1.1
Advanced degree	43.7	16.5	10.2	23.8	5.6

NOTE: Percentages may not sum to 100 percent due to rounding.

SOURCE: National Center for Education Statistics, High School & Beyond: Sophomore Cohort 1980–1992

The 1980 high school sophomores not only were more likely to attain a postsecondary credential if they enrolled in postsecondary education immediately after high school but they were also more likely to earn a degree if they enrolled immediately and full time (table 4). At the 4-year institutions, for example, almost 58 percent of 1980 sophomores who enrolled full time in fall 1982 had earned a bachelor's degree by 1992, compared with about one-fourth of those who enrolled part time. Similarly, students who enrolled immediately and full time at 2-year institutions had higher rates of postsecondary attainment: one-fourth of students who enrolled in a 2-year public institution full time in fall 1982 had earned a bachelor's degree by 1992, compared with 14 percent of those who enrolled part time. Likewise, 24 percent of those who enrolled immediately and full time in a 2-year public institution had earned an associate's degree by 1992, while 9 percent of those who enrolled part time in fall 1982 had attained an associate's degree.

Table 4
Percentage of 1980 high school sophomores by highest degree attained through 1992, by timing and intensity of initial postsecondary enrollment

Type of start in postsecondary education	Highest degree through 1992							
	Less than high school graduate	High school	Certi-ficate	Assoc-iate's	Bachelor's	Master's	Profes-sional	Doctorate
Total	5.8	51.5	11.0	7.9	20.0	2.7	0.9	0.16
4-year institution								
Full-time fall 1982	*	21.2	3.5	4.6	57.8	9.0	3.4	0.5
Part-time fall 1982	0.0	52.2	6.7	10.0	27.2	3.5	0.1	0.4
Delayed entry	0.4	55.6	8.1	7.37	24.0	3.7	0.4	0.4
2-year public institution								
Full-time fall 1982	0.3	36.5	11.9	24.4	24.6	2.1	0.2	0.0
Part-time fall 1982	1.6	59.5	13.4	9.4	14.4	0.9	0.8	*
Delayed entry	1.7	63.0	16.9	12.0	6.2	0.2	0.0	0.0
Other institution								
Fall 1982	0.2	23.0	34.3	24.5	15.7	1.9	0.4	0.0
Delayed entry	1.9	31.4	48.4	14.4	3.8	0.1	0.1	0.0
Other enrollment	0.0	0.0	86.5	5.1	6.0	1.1	0.4	0.8
No enrollment	16.1	83.9	0.0	0.0	0.0	0.0	0.0	0.0

* Indicates less than 0.1 percent.
NOTE: Percentages may not sum to 100 percent due to rounding.

SOURCE: National Center for Education Statistics, High School & Beyond: Sophomore Cohort 1980–1992

Interestingly, the rate at which students attained some type of postsecondary degree was about the same among immediate part-time entrants to postsecondary education as among those who delayed entry. At 4-year institutions, for example, 27 percent of immediate part-time entrants had attained a bachelor's degree by 1992, compared with 24 percent of those who delayed entry. Students who enrolled part time in 2-year institutions in fall 1982 were more likely than delayed entrants to earn a bachelor's degree, but rates of completion were about the same for both groups with regard to associate's degrees and vocational certificates.

These patterns suggest that differences in attainment may not be as much due to differences in the timing of entry as they are due to differences in the intensity of students' initial enrollment. There are many plausible reasons why one might find differences in attainment between those who enroll immediately full time and those who do not. One possibility is that those who enroll full time right after high school are more committed to postsecondary education than are other students, and therefore are more likely to complete a degree and attain their goals. Alternatively, the timing and intensity of students' initial enrollments may reflect other characteristics, such as financial capacity or the presence of outside distractions (such as family obligations, work demands, or the proximity of noncollege-bound friends), that affect students' inclination and opportunity to complete a degree and attain their goals.

Length of Initial Delay

The fact that students who delayed entry into postsecondary education were less likely to attain a credential may, in part, reflect the length of time they delayed their entry rather than delay per se. Long delays after high school would allow less time for completing longer term degrees within the 10-year period covered by the fourth followup. Although the data are somewhat ambiguous on this point, they do not appear to support this interpretation. Longer delays were associated with lower levels of attainment, and this was true whether the student's initial enrollment was in a 4-year or a 2-year public institution (table 5). Furthermore, the average length of delay, controlling for attainment, was the same regardless of the type of institution in which the student initially enrolled. These results suggest that long delays adversely affect attainment. It is still possible that students who delayed their enrollment did not have time to finish their degree within the 10-year period, but other data on length of delay also are not consistent with this interpretation.[10]

---

[10]The effects of "time censoring"--that is, arbitrarily limiting the period of educational attainment to the 10-year time frame of the fourth followup--cannot wholly be ruled out, but it does not appear to explain the lower levels of attainment among those who delayed their entry into postsecondary education. Only about 5 percent of the 1980 sophomores entered postsecondary education after June 1986 (see table 2.2 in the Compendium), so most postsecondary activity among this cohort took place before then. Nonetheless, about 5 percent of the sophomores did claim that their major activity in 1992 was taking undergraduate courses, and another 2 percent claimed to be enrolled in vocational/technical courses (see table 1.3 in the Compendium). It is possible that the findings with regard to the effects of delayed entry could be altered by the educational outcomes for these groups, but the relatively small number of students involved makes this unlikely.

Table 5
Average length of initial delay (in months) among 1980 high school sophomores who delayed entry into postsecondary education, by highest degree attained through 1992 and type of institution

Type of institution	Average length of delay (months)	Average length of delay in months by highest degree through 1992				
		High school	Certi-ficate	Assoc-iate's	Bachelor's	Advanced degree
Total	13.9	18.9	22.7	12.4	5.5	4.9
4-year	28.8	33.3	28.8	29.4	19.4	—
2-year public	33.9	36.5	30.8	30.6	20.6	—

—Sample size is too small for a reliable estimate.

NOTE: The total line includes both immediate entrants and delayed entrants.

SOURCE: National Center for Education Statistics, High School & Beyond: Sophomore Cohort 1980–1992

The length of delay before initial entry into postsecondary education was strongly associated with students' postsecondary expectations while still in high school. Students with lower postsecondary expectations in 1982 delayed their entry longer than those who had higher aspirations (table 6). Students who in 1982 had no plans to pursue postsecondary education waited

Table 6
Average length of initial delay before entering postsecondary education (in months) among 1980 high school sophomores, by highest degree attained through 1992 and postsecondary expectations

Postsecondary expectations (1982)	Average length of delay (months)	Average length of delay in months by highest degree through 1992				
		High school	Certi-ficate	Assoc-iate's	Bachelor's	Advanced degree
Total	13.9	18.9	22.7	12.4	5.5	4.9
None	37.6	38.4	39.1	32.1	—	—
Vocational-technical	20.5	22.4	23.0	14.3	11.9	—
Less than four-year degree	13.2	17.4	16.1	8.2	6.6	5.8
College degree	8.2	12.1	17.6	9.0	4.7	4.3
Advanced degree	6.7	9.6	8.7	10.6	5.0	4.8

—Sample size is too small for a reliable estimate.

SOURCE: National Center for Education Statistics, High School & Beyond: Sophomore Cohort 1980–1992

9

an average of 38 months before enrolling in a postsecondary institution, compared with an average of 13 months for those who intended to obtain a less-than-4-year degree or 8 months for those who planned to pursue a bachelor's degree.

Length of delay was also associated in expected ways with students' socioeconomic status (SES) and academic achievement in high school (table 7). Low SES students tended to delay their entry into postsecondary education longer than those in the middle two quartiles, and those in the middle two quartiles tended to delay longer than did high SES students. Furthermore, this pattern was evident at each level of postsecondary attainment. Similarly, students with lower achievement test scores in high school delayed entry into postsecondary education considerably longer than did students with high test scores.

Table 7
Average length of initial delay before entering postsecondary education (in months) among 1980 high school sophomores, by highest degree attained through 1992, socioeconomic status quartile, and test score quartile

Student characteristic	Average length of delay (months)	Average length of delay in months by highest degree through 1992				
		High school	Certi- ficate	Assoc- iate's	Bachelor's	Advanced degree
Total	13.9	18.9	22.7	12.4	5.5	4.9
Socioeconomic status						
Low quartile	21.5	23.8	29.2	15.2	7.7	—
Middle two quartiles	14.3	19.8	20.2	11.5	5.6	4.5
High quartile	7.9	11.8	15.2	9.5	4.9	4.9
Test score composite (1982)						
Low quartile	24.6	24.6	31.4	17.0	8.2	—
Middle two quartiles	14.2	17.8	19.7	11.3	6.0	4.9
High quartile	7.3	12.7	16.7	7.6	4.8	4.2

—Sample size is too small for a reliable estimate.

SOURCE: National Center for Education Statistics, High School & Beyond: Sophomore Cohort 1980–1992

It should be noted that within each SES and test score quartile, lower levels of attainment were strongly associated with longer delays. In other words, although length of delay is likely to be greater among students with lower SES and achievement, there is still a very strong independent association between delay and attainment. This finding is important because it suggests that realizing improvements in rates of postsecondary attainment may depend on strategies for decreasing delay of entry, regardless of other variables (such as student demographics) that are strongly associated with attainment.

Time to Degree

Another critical variable in understanding variation in the levels of postsecondary attainment among the 1980 high school sophomores is the time students took to complete a credential once they enrolled in some type of postsecondary institution. As one would expect, the time to degree attainment from first postsecondary enrollment to completion of a degree varied by the type of degree earned (table 8). For example, the average time needed to complete a vocational certificate was 30 months, the average time to complete an associate's degree was just over 36 months, and the average time to a bachelor's degree was 56 months.

Table 8
Average number of months between first enrollment and attainment of degrees, by type of degree, postsecondary expectations, and timing and intensity of initial postsecondary enrollment

Postsecondary education characteristics	Certi-ficate	Assoc-iate's	Bachelor's
Total	29.6	36.8	55.7
Postsecondary expectations			
None	18.6	30.7	—
Vocational-technical	20.0	29.9	60.8
Less than 4-year degree	36.4	36.3	61.6
College degree	44.2	39.8	55.7
Advanced degree	44.8	43.5	53.5
Type of start in postsecondary education			
4-year institution			
Full-time fall 1982	57.2	47.0	53.1
Part-time fall 1982	—	—	71.1
Delayed entry	36.4	41.1	48.9
2-year institution			
Full-time fall 1982	43.4	34.6	66.5
Part-time fall 1982	37.6	55.7	67.6
Delayed entry	32.5	38.0	66.9
Other institution			
Fall 1982	19.4	27.8	58.5
Delayed entry	16.5	28.7	—

—Sample size is too small for a reliable estimate.

SOURCE: National Center for Education Statistics, High School & Beyond: Sophomore Cohort 1980–1992

The time to complete a degree, holding degree types constant, varied by postsecondary expectations. In general, students whose first enrollment was in an institution that offered the type of degree that they expected to earn took less time to complete their degree than did those who

11

changed their plans. While this finding may seem obvious, the effects of changing plans were more pronounced among students who expected to earn a bachelor's or advanced degree but ultimately completed a vocational certificate or associate's degree, than among students who completed a degree that was higher than what they had expected to earn while in high school.[11]

For example, students who earned a vocational certificate when their postsecondary goal was a bachelor's degree took, on average, 24 months longer from first enrollment to completion than those who started out with a vocational degree as their objective. However, there was no significant difference in the time required to earn a bachelor's degree between those who planned to earn a vocational certificate and those who set to earn a bachelor's degree. Most likely, students who initially enrolled in a 4-year or public 2-year institution pursued a bachelor's or associate's degree for some time before realizing that their interests or abilities lay elsewhere; thus, the total amount of time enrolled was considerably greater than the amount of time typically required to earn the vocational certificate or associate's degree they eventually received.[12] This finding is important because it underscores the fact that changing one's postsecondary course of study can involve a considerable loss of time. Hence, strategies that help students better hone their postsecondary objectives and that help students to achieve these objectives may have significant payoffs.

Not surprisingly, time to completion was closely associated with whether or not students enrolled full time or part time. Students who enrolled full time in 4-year institutions completed a bachelor's degree in 53 months, compared with 71 months for those enrolled part time. Full-time students in 2-year institutions finished an associate's degree in 35 months on average, while part-time students took an average of 56 months . However, when students enrolled initially in a 2-year institution and subsequently completed a bachelor's degree, there were no differences among full-time, part-time, or delayed-entry students in the average time to completion. For all three groups, completing a bachelor's degree took about 67 months. Immediate, full-time entrants to the public 2-year institutions were more likely to earn a bachelor's degree than were those who entered immediately part time or who delayed their entry, but it took all of these students about the same amount of time to attain a bachelor's degree if they succeeded in completing one.

Attainment and Number of Institutions Attended

On average, students who completed a bachelor's degree (excluding advanced degree recipients) attended more institutions than did those who earned an associate's degree or a vocational certificate (table 9). But these differences were due more to the relatively large number of students who transferred from a public 2-year or other institution to a 4-year institution than to

---

[11]The degree attainment categories used here are not mutually exclusive, and the certificate earned by those who planned to get an associate's degree or higher may not be either the first or the highest degree they attained.

[12]The disparity in the amount of time taken to earn a vocational certificate between those who start out expecting to earn a bachelor's or advanced degree and those who start with a vocational objective is consistent with the literature on "reverse transfer" students, those students who transfer from a 4-year to a 2-year-or-less institution. Based on an analysis of the high school classes of 1972 and 1980, Grubb concludes that ". . . reverse transfer is not an especially successful route to completing credentials, even compared to the experiences of those students starting in 2-year institutions." Four years after high school, reverse transfer students tended to have low completion rates compared with students in 2-year public institutions, presumably because they were still enrolled, and a large percentage of them (almost 40 percent) left higher education without completing a credential of any type. See W. Norton Grubb, *Access, Achievement, Completion, and "Milling Around" in Postsecondary Vocational Education* (Berkeley, CA: MPR Associates, Inc., April 1989), 33.

the behavior of students who initially enrolled in a 4-year institution. The average number of institutions attended by bachelor's degree recipients whose initial enrollment was in a 4-year institution (either immediate or delayed) was consistently less than the number of institutions attended by bachelor's degree recipients who started in a public 2-year or other institution. Likewise, students whose initial enrollment was in a 4-year institution full time in fall 1982 and who earned a vocational certificate or associate's degree generally attended more institutions than did those whose degree more closely paralleled their initial enrollment.

Table 9
Average number of postsecondary institutions attended by highest degree attained through 1992, by timing and intensity of initial postsecondary enrollment

Type of start in postsecondary education	Certi-ficate	Assoc-iate's	Bachelor's
Total	1.5	1.4	1.7
4-year institution			
Full-time fall 1982	2.3	2.0	1.5
Part-time fall 1982	—	—	2.2
Delayed entry	1.9	1.6	1.4
2-year institution			
Full-time fall 1982	1.7	1.3	2.3
Part-time fall 1982	1.7	1.6	2.4
Delayed entry	1.6	1.3	2.3
Other institution			
Fall 1982	1.2	1.3	2.1
Delayed entry	1.1	1.3	—

—Sample size is too small for a reliable estimate.

SOURCE: National Center for Education Statistics, High School & Beyond: Sophomore Cohort 1980–1992

Findings and Conclusions

Members of the 1980 sophomore class who set high goals in high school tended to have higher average levels of educational attainment 10 years after leaving high school than did those who had lower postsecondary expectations. In addition, a key finding was that the odds of earning a bachelor's degree or higher change when entry into postsecondary education is delayed. Those who entered postsecondary education immediately full time were much more likely to earn a bachelor's degree or higher than were students who entered part time in fall 1982 or who delayed their entry into postsecondary education. This was true regardless of students' level of SES or their performance on standardized tests. Furthermore, the longer students delayed their entry into postsecondary education, the lower their average levels of educational attainment. Among those students who delayed entry for longer than about 1 year after high school, only one in ten attained a bachelor's degree or higher by 1992.

The length of delay in entering postsecondary education and the time needed to complete a degree influence the differences in rates of attainment between those who enter postsecondary education and those who wait. Nevertheless, the mere act of delay appears to be strongly associated with the lower likelihood of completing a postsecondary credential, especially a bachelor's degree or higher. Thus, while a future followup of this cohort would probably show an increase in attainment among those who delayed entry simply because more time would have passed, it is very unlikely that future rates would ever approach those who began postsecondary education immediately after high school, especially if they enrolled full time.

Table Compendium

Section 1

Where Did They Start
And Where Are They Now?

Descriptive Characteristics of the 1980 Sophomore Class in 1992

- Educational aspirations of the 1980 sophomores in 1982 (when most of them were high school seniors) were related to their socioeconomic status (SES). Those in the lowest SES quartile were far more likely to expect no postsecondary education than were those in the middle two and highest quartiles. On the other hand, students in the highest quartile were much more likely than the other groups to expect college or graduate school (table 1.1).

- The 1980 sophomores' high school grades were positively associated with their SES: as grades increased, so too did sophomores' average SES. Test scores were positively associated with 1980 family income, high school grades, and parents' educational attainment (table 1.2).

Major Activities of the 1980 Sophomore Class in 1992

- Seventy-nine percent of 1980 high school sophomores reported that working was their primary activity during the week before they were surveyed in 1992. About 1 in 10 were enrolled in either a training or an academic educational program, and around 1 in 20 reported being laid off, looking for work, or both (table 1.3).

- Respondents whose mothers worked were neither more nor less likely to be working themselves than those whose mothers did not work. Moreover, the employment rates of 1980 high school sophomores did not vary by the intensity of their mothers' employment (full- or part-time) or by the timing of their mothers' employment (before elementary school, during elementary school, or during high school) (table 1.3).

- Employment rates varied by race–ethnicity. More than twice the percentage of blacks (8 percent) than of whites (3 percent) reported that they were looking for work the week before they were surveyed, and a larger percentage of whites than of blacks reported that they were working during that week. Among Hispanics, the percentages of those who were working and of those who were looking for work the week before they were surveyed did not differ significantly from those of whites (table 1.3).

Volunteer Activities of the 1980 Sophomore Class

- The percentage of 1980 high school sophomores who reported spending time engaged in volunteer work in 1992 was small. Even if one assumes that no respondents reported spending time in more than one activity, almost two-thirds (65 percent) of the cohort did not participate in any volunteer activities (table 1.4).

- Participation in voluntary activities varied by gender. Women reported involvement in church and education groups at a higher rate than did, while males were more likely than females to report spending time in sports groups (table 1.4).

- For married respondents, another factor affecting participation in volunteer activities was the presence of children in the family. Married 1980 sophomores with children were more likely to participate in education groups, youth clubs, or both than those without children. The presence of children was not significantly related to participation in these groups among unmarried respondents (table 1.4).

Table 1.1—Percentage distribution of 1980 high school sophomores, by educational aspirations in 1982 and selected characteristics

Student characteristics	Educational aspirations				
	High school	Vocational/ technical	Some college	College degree	Advanced degree
Total	24.4	20.6	18.0	20.6	16.6
High school diploma status in 1982					
Regular diploma	18.9	20.3	18.7	23.3	18.7
Diploma returned	35.0	28.2	18.5	10.9	7.4
Returned no diploma	46.8	27.4	16.7	3.5	5.7
No return	65.3	18.8	7.7	3.3	4.8
Father's 1982 after-high-school aspirations for children					
Go to college	6.0	10.3	21.4	34.2	28.1
Full-time job	56.7	26.4	10.2	3.5	3.2
Trade school	19.6	65.8	9.4	2.8	2.4
Military service	36.0	29.5	14.3	12.3	7.9
Mother's 1982 after-high-school aspirations for children					
Go to college	6.6	10.9	22.4	33.2	26.9
Full-time job	60.9	24.4	9.4	2.9	2.4
Trade school	19.7	70.4	6.6	1.9	1.4
Military service	40.6	28.6	12.8	11.3	6.8
Occupational aspiration for age 30 in 1982					
Clerical	33.2	32.9	24.3	7.5	2.2
Craftsman	44.0	45.2	7.5	2.6	0.7
Farmer	42.7	24.7	13.7	14.5	4.4
Homemaker	58.0	17.6	12.6	8.6	3.2
Laborer	69.5	17.6	9.5	2.3	1.1
Manager	12.8	16.7	24.0	29.6	16.8
Military	41.8	24.0	9.6	16.5	8.2
Operative	59.8	27.5	8.9	2.6	1.2
Professional	8.7	11.7	19.7	35.5	24.3
Professional/doctor	5.5	4.2	6.3	18.1	65.9
Proprietor/owner	29.2	28.7	21.9	14.4	5.9
Protective service	29.1	17.4	33.0	14.8	5.7
Sales	25.7	18.4	19.6	30.9	5.5
School teacher	7.4	3.3	15.6	48.9	24.8
Service	36.5	42.1	12.0	5.7	3.8
Technical	9.8	23.8	28.6	24.4	13.4
Time watching TV (weekdays) in 1982					
No TV weekdays	22.4	19.2	15.9	20.2	22.3
Less than 1 hour	17.2	20.3	15.2	24.2	23.1
1–2 hours	19.8	20.2	18.8	21.7	19.5
2–3 hours	22.2	21.2	18.4	21.6	16.6
3–4 hours	24.5	20.6	17.7	23.4	13.8
4–5 hours	31.7	21.1	17.0	18.1	12.2
5 hours or more	35.8	21.1	17.3	15.0	10.8
Socioeconomic status (1980)					
Low quartile	40.7	26.6	15.2	11.3	6.1
Middle two quartiles	22.3	22.6	20.2	21.0	13.8
High quartile	7.4	9.7	16.2	32.2	34.5

NOTE: Percentages may not sum to 100 percent due to rounding.
SOURCE: National Center for Education Statistics, High School & Beyond: 1980 Sophomore Cohort, 1980–1992.

Table 1.2—Average percentile rank of 1980 high school sophomores on specified composite scales, by selected characteristics

Student characteristics	Socio-economic status (1980)	Test scores (1982)	Self-concept (1982)	Locus of control (1982)	Community orientation (1982)
Total	50.7	49.6	50.1	49.1	48.2
Sex					
Male	52.5	50.4	50.2	48.6	50.8
Female	48.9	48.8	50.1	49.7	45.7
Race–ethnicity					
Native American/Alaska Native	40.3	35.1	51.1	42.0	54.3
Asian/Pacific Islander	53.8	54.1	53.2	50.3	55.8
Black	35.6	26.7	49.3	46.5	60.7
White	54.4	54.7	49.3	49.5	44.2
Hispanic-Mexican	32.2	32.8	52.1	42.5	55.9
Hispanic-Cuban	48.3	45.7	51.4	50.3	50.6
Hispanic-Puerto Rican	29.9	28.2	47.9	41.8	56.6
Hispanic-other	42.4	33.0	51.5	42.9	54.4
Family income in 1980					
Less than $8,000	24.7	31.9	53.6	44.5	54.0
$8,000–$14,999	33.9	43.4	49.3	43.9	47.4
$15,000–$19,999	42.0	48.9	47.5	46.1	45.8
$20,000–$24,999	48.7	53.1	48.3	47.7	46.0
$25,000–$29,999	54.8	55.1	47.4	50.2	43.9
$30,000–$39,999	62.0	58.1	46.1	50.3	43.0
$40,000–$49,999	69.1	61.2	45.1	51.6	43.1
$50,000 or more	78.9	63.7	43.6	53.6	45.4
Father's occupation in 1980					
Technical	69.8	57.7	45.5	49.7	45.9
Clerical	62.2	51.1	49.8	46.6	46.4
Craftsman	39.4	45.8	50.2	47.1	46.3
Farmer	40.1	45.8	49.9	43.3	43.9
Laborer	25.7	43.8	49.1	46.9	48.8
Manager	74.6	61.5	47.2	52.8	44.8
Military	53.0	48.1	43.5	50.2	51.5
Operative	32.6	43.5	51.5	46.8	46.9
Professional	78.4	63.0	47.5	55.4	45.3
Professional/doctor	89.9	74.8	43.8	57.4	46.9
Proprietor/owner	65.1	55.3	48.7	55.6	48.1
Protective service	56.2	54.8	50.2	51.0	48.7
Sales	69.9	61.1	45.4	53.0	45.0
School teacher	81.2	66.6	43.5	59.2	46.1
Service	31.7	44.5	50.7	49.2	52.0
Program in high school					
General	45.4	41.7	54.1	46.1	47.9
Academic	60.8	64.2	44.3	55.0	46.9
Vocational	39.7	34.2	52.8	42.0	48.5
Urbanicity of high school area					
Urban	45.8	43.3	50.9	48.4	53.4
Suburban	55.9	53.1	49.8	50.6	47.0
Rural	45.8	48.1	50.2	47.3	46.5

Table 1.2—Average percentile rank of 1980 high school sophomores on specified composite scales, by selected characteristics—Continued

Student characteristics	Socio-economic status (1980)	Test scores (1982)	Self-concept (1982)	Locus of control (1982)	Community orientation (1982)
Community lived in Feb. 1982					
Rural/farm	43.3	47.8	47.7	42.5	42.4
Small city	51.6	52.2	46.0	45.2	42.6
Medium city	52.3	49.7	44.9	43.6	43.3
Suburb medium city	58.1	52.0	44.8	45.9	42.1
Large city	48.8	47.2	44.3	44.1	46.4
Suburb large city	65.4	63.3	44.5	48.3	40.2
Huge city	49.7	50.8	40.9	45.2	49.0
Suburb huge city	67.1	66.0	39.9	51.7	42.3
Military base	46.4	47.0	41.6	41.5	49.7
Religious background in 1980					
Baptist	42.3	41.7	48.2	47.2	51.6
Methodist	56.2	54.3	47.2	51.4	46.9
Lutheran	57.3	58.9	46.3	49.6	42.9
Presbyterian	60.8	56.6	46.3	51.9	45.8
Episcopalian	71.1	65.3	43.2	50.9	45.7
Other protestant	55.1	61.6	51.2	54.3	45.7
Catholic	53.5	54.8	49.1	49.5	45.3
Other Christian	49.2	48.4	52.3	50.3	48.5
Jewish	76.3	71.2	43.0	56.6	50.0
Other religion	41.2	39.6	48.7	46.5	46.9
None	44.2	44.9	53.4	45.4	45.1
Political beliefs in 1980					
Conservative	56.5	56.8	44.8	51.7	49.1
Moderate	55.5	57.8	45.5	52.4	47.6
Liberal	56.4	59.1	47.0	53.5	48.6
Radical	50.9	48.1	47.2	47.4	48.9
None	45.1	43.8	53.3	45.7	45.6
Grades in high school					
Mostly A 90–100	64.6	81.5	40.5	62.2	44.6
Half A/B 85–89	60.6	72.1	44.0	58.7	45.3
Mostly B 80–84	55.3	60.7	47.2	52.5	45.4
Half B/C 75–79	49.3	46.1	50.0	48.4	47.7
Mostly C 70–74	44.7	35.7	53.7	44.1	50.2
Half C/D 65–69	40.5	27.3	54.4	40.8	51.0
Mostly D 60–64	35.7	21.7	62.5	43.0	57.4
Parents' educational attainment in 1980					
High school	37.4	43.7	51.5	45.6	46.9
Vocational/technical	51.4	52.1	47.8	50.2	46.8
Some college	68.3	59.4	47.4	53.3	46.8
Bachelor's degree	82.2	66.2	44.3	55.7	44.5
Advanced degree	88.0	68.1	43.1	53.6	45.9

SOURCE: National Center for Eduction Statistics, High School & Beyond: 1980 Sophomore Cohort, 1980–1992.

Table 1.3—Percentage distribution of 1980 high school sophomores who reported the following as their major activity or activities in 1992, by selected characteristics

Student characteristics	Working	Layoff	Looking for work	Taking break	Training program	Vocational/ technical courses	Undergraduate academic courses	Graduate/ professional courses	Active duty/armed forces
Total	79.3	1.3	3.9	2.9	0.2	2.0	5.4	3.3	0.8
Language spoken at home in 1982									
Single non-English language	78.7	0.5	5.1	4.1	0.4	2.5	5.2	4.7	1.9
Non-English language dominant	80.0	1.3	2.3	4.0	1.2	2.2	3.5	2.4	0.9
Combination of languages	78.9	1.1	3.9	2.7	0.4	1.9	7.8	4.6	0.3
English is the dominant language	80.4	1.0	3.5	2.8	0.1	1.8	5.5	3.1	0.9
Marital status in 1992									
Married	78.1	1.2	1.6	2.8	0.3	2.0	4.5	2.3	0.8
Separated	68.6	4.0	6.4	0.6	0.0	4.8	5.0	2.2	0.5
Divorced	79.9	1.5	6.7	1.9	0.6	2.4	7.6	3.6	1.2
Widowed	—	—	—	—	—	—	—	—	—
Never married	81.2	1.2	6.2	3.3	0.1	1.9	6.5	4.6	0.7
Living in a marriage-like relationship	86.8	0.5	6.5	1.6	0.0	0.7	1.0	1.7	0.0
Before elementary school mother worked									
Did not work	80.4	1.1	3.1	3.2	0.2	1.3	5.1	3.9	0.9
Part-time work	83.5	0.6	3.0	1.6	0.2	2.2	7.6	3.4	0.9
Full-time work	80.8	0.9	3.8	2.9	0.3	2.7	5.8	2.8	0.5
In elementary school mother worked									
Did not work	80.4	1.0	2.9	3.1	0.2	1.2	5.3	3.9	0.8
Part-time work	82.3	1.1	3.5	2.7	0.2	1.7	5.7	3.2	1.2
Full-time work	79.8	0.9	3.6	2.8	0.2	2.6	6.1	2.8	0.7
In high school mother worked									
Did not work	79.3	1.0	3.1	3.2	0.3	1.3	5.4	3.4	0.6
Part-time work	80.9	1.0	4.0	2.8	0.0	1.6	5.4	4.1	0.9
Full-time work	81.1	0.9	3.3	2.5	0.3	2.3	6.0	2.9	1.0
Race-ethnicity									
Native American/Alaska Native	77.0	1.6	7.1	2.2	0.0	1.2	4.7	3.4	0.2
Asian/Pacific Islander	75.7	0.3	3.1	7.3	0.8	2.0	5.4	6.3	1.1
Black	73.3	1.2	7.6	3.9	0.7	2.4	6.0	1.6	1.5
Hispanic	77.4	1.8	4.6	2.5	0.2	2.0	5.3	1.4	0.9
White	80.6	1.2	3.0	2.8	0.2	1.9	5.5	3.8	0.7

—Sample size is too small for a reliable estimate.

NOTES: Activities reported for week prior to survey in 1992. The percentage of students who reported working or looking for work differs from table 3.1.A due to a difference in timing (table 3.1.A refers to February 1992) and patterns of missing data. Percentages may not sum to 100 percent due to rounding.

SOURCE: National Center for Education Statistics, High School & Beyond: 1980 Sophomore Cohort, 1980–1992.

Table 1.4—Percentage of 1980 high school sophomores who reported spending time in various unpaid activities in 1992, by selected characteristics

Student characteristics	Church groups	Education groups	Organized volunteer	Political groups	Service clubs	Sports groups	Union trade professional	Youth clubs
Total	11.1	5.7	4.3	1.1	4.0	2.6	1.1	5.3
Sex								
Male	9.5	3.1	3.5	1.1	4.4	3.4	1.3	5.6
Female	12.7	8.1	5.0	1.2	3.7	1.8	1.0	5.0
Marital and parental status in 1992								
Married no children	12.0	4.0	3.9	1.5	5.1	2.6	1.7	3.8
Married with children	14.9	7.7	3.6	0.6	3.1	2.5	0.9	6.8
Divorced/sep/widow no children	7.4	2.1	7.6	0.2	3.7	0.7	0.2	2.5
Divorced/sep/widow with children	8.1	7.9	3.3	0.7	2.8	3.0	0.2	6.5
Never married no children	7.6	3.8	5.5	1.8	4.9	3.0	1.5	4.2
Never married with children	9.0	7.4	3.1	1.3	3.6	1.9	0.7	6.0
Living together no children	1.2	0.1	3.4	0.0	0.0	3.4	0.0	1.0
Living together with children	11.3	5.4	0.0	0.0	2.3	7.1	4.4	8.5
Highest degree earned by 1992								
Less than high school	6.0	5.4	1.4	0.9	2.5	4.4	1.9	4.3
High school	9.8	5.5	3.2	0.8	3.5	2.2	0.7	5.2
Certificate	13.0	5.5	5.0	1.0	3.1	2.3	0.9	5.6
Associate's	13.3	4.5	6.2	1.0	3.1	1.8	1.3	4.6
Bachelor's	14.1	5.5	6.4	2.1	5.7	3.1	1.9	5.6
Master's	12.5	13.9	7.0	2.8	9.2	4.4	2.8	5.0
Professional	9.7	7.3	4.6	3.3	8.1	3.9	2.0	10.0
Doctorate	—	—	—	—	—	—	—	—
Locus of control (1982)								
Low quartile	8.7	5.2	3.6	0.8	3.5	2.3	0.7	4.9
Middle two quartiles	12.1	5.6	4.5	1.2	4.2	2.6	1.3	5.7
High quartile	11.6	6.2	4.5	1.5	4.2	2.9	1.2	5.0

—Sample size is too small for a reliable estimate.

NOTE: The activity categories are not exclusive.

SOURCE: National Center for Education Statistics, High School & Beyond: 1980 Sophomore Cohort, 1980–1992.

22

Section 2

Educational Experiences
of the 1980 Sophomore Class

Differences in Attainment

- Educational expectations in high school were clearly related to educational attainment 10 years later, but sophomores' expectations may be set well before they get to high school. Differences in attainment were related to expectations that were set as early as the sixth grade. A greater percentage of those who had decided to attend college in sixth grade enrolled in a 4-year institution after high school than of those who had decided against college, were not sure, or had not thought about it (table 2.1).

- Females were more likely to enroll immediately in either a 4- or 2-year college, and were more likely to have enrolled in some type of postsecondary institution before 1992 than were males (table 2.3). However, males and females were equally likely to have attained a bachelor's, master's, or doctoral degree by 1992. Males were more likely than females to have earned a professional degree (table 2.4.A).

- Nearly three out of four 1980 high school sophomores in the lowest SES quartile had no postsecondary degrees by 1992, and this group was significantly less likely to graduate from high school or to attain a bachelor's degree or higher than 1980 sophomores in the middle two and upper SES quartiles. Those in the middle two SES quartiles were less likely to attain a bachelor's degree or higher than those in the highest quartile (table 2.4.A).

- The same patterns of attainment that were apparent by SES appear when the sample is divided by test score quartiles.[11] Those in the lowest quartile were less likely to finish high school or attain a degree beyond high school than those in the middle two or highest. Respondents in the highest quartile were more likely to have earned bachelor's degrees or higher than those in the middle two quartiles (table 2.4.A).

- The timing of 1980 sophomores' entry into postsecondary education was significantly related to their levels of educational attainment. Those who entered a postsecondary institution after October 1982 were more likely to have attained only a high school diploma or vocational certificate by 1992 than were those who entered immediately; however, those who entered immediately were more likely to have attained a bachelor's or advanced degree by 1992 (tables 2.4.B & 2.4.C).

---

[11]The similarity of the relationship between attainment and SES and attainment and test scores is due to the high correlation between SES and test scores. The Pearson correlation between these two variables is 0.775.

23

- The intensity of initial attendance at a postsecondary institution was related to degree attainment. Respondents who attended either a 4-year or public 2-year school immediately after high school were more likely to attain bachelor's degrees if they enrolled full time than if they enrolled part time. By contrast, those who enrolled part time were more likely to have no credential beyond a high school diploma than those who enrolled full time (table 2.4.A).

Graduate School Admissions

- While about two-thirds (68 percent) of bachelor's degree recipients took graduate or professional admissions exams, fewer than half (31 percent) actually applied to a graduate or professional institution. The small number of respondents who applied to graduate schools and the large number who were accepted at the school of their choice implies a strong degree of self-selection throughout the graduate school application process (table 2.9).

- Bachelor's degree recipients who borrowed money for their undergraduate education were three times as likely to take graduate or professional admissions exams as were those who had not borrowed. However, those who had borrowed money applied to graduate school at only one-third the rate of those who had not borrowed. Of those who applied, those who borrowed money and those who did not were equally likely to be accepted at their first-choice institution. Among those who borrowed, the amount borrowed did not affect the rate of participation in graduate admissions tests, the application rate, or the rate of acceptance into a graduate program (table 2.9).

Table 2.1–Percentage distribution of 1980 high school sophomores by type of postsecondary institution in which they first enrolled, by selected characteristics

Student characteristics	Never enrolled	Private for-profit	Private not-for-profit less-than-4-year	Public less-than-2-year	Public 2-year	Public 4-year	Private not-for-profit 4-year
Total	33.6	6.1	1.4	3.5	26.7	19.5	9.3
College expectations in sixth grade							
Decided to go	16.6	4.9	1.5	2.8	25.8	32.5	15.9
Planned not to go	52.3	7.2	1.4	4.2	24.3	7.7	2.9
Not sure	34.3	6.8	1.7	3.8	29.0	17.9	6.5
Hadn't thought about it	28.5	6.5	1.5	4.8	30.6	19.5	8.7
Postsecondary expectations in 1982							
None	73.1	4.5	0.5	2.7	15.6	2.6	1.0
Vocational/technical	41.1	14.0	2.0	7.2	29.5	4.8	1.4
Less-than-4-year degree	21.4	6.2	2.3	2.2	45.3	16.5	6.1
College degree	8.0	2.8	1.2	2.8	26.7	40.6	17.9
Advanced degree	6.6	1.8	1.4	2.7	20.6	42.6	24.4
First institution start date							
Never enrolled	100.0	0.0	0.0	0.0	0.0	0.0	0.0
Before November 1982	0.0	5.5	2.2	3.8	33.0	37.3	18.2
Nov. 1982–May 1983	0.0	17.6	1.6	8.2	54.6	11.9	6.1
June 1983–May 1984	0.0	14.8	3.3	7.3	47.9	19.1	7.6
June 1984–May 1986	0.0	21.8	2.4	10.7	46.6	13.4	5.1
June 1986 or later	0.0	18.3	1.7	8.8	53.9	12.6	4.6
Number of applications to college in 1982							
Did not apply	53.6	7.5	0.9	4.4	25.9	5.8	2.0
1 college	8.9	5.2	1.7	2.6	32.7	37.1	11.8
2–3 colleges	4.7	3.0	2.4	3.1	22.2	42.7	21.8
4 or more colleges	4.1	1.6	1.5	1.6	11.2	37.4	42.7
Accepted at 1982 first-choice college							
No applications	59.8	6.7	0.8	3.5	24.1	3.8	1.3
Attended first choice	0.0	5.6	2.5	3.5	29.8	40.3	18.5
Accepted but did not attend	21.4	5.9	1.1	4.5	36.4	21.0	9.7
Was not accepted at first choice	11.3	4.5	1.5	2.6	25.8	28.5	25.9

NOTES: Institution types are defined by degree offerings (less-than-2-year, 2- to 3-year, 4-year or more) and control (public, private not-for-profit, and private for-profit). Percentages may not sum to 100 percent due to rounding.
SOURCE: National Center for Education Statistics, High School & Beyond: 1980 Sophomore Cohort, 1980–1992.

Table 2.2—Percentage distribution of 1980 high school sophomores by the timing of their first postsecondary enrollment, by selected characteristics

Student characteristics	Never enrolled	Before November 1982	November 1982– May 1983	June 1983– May 1984	June 1984– May 1985	June 1985– May 1986	June 1986– May 1987	June 1987– May 1988	June 1988– May 1989	June 1989– May 1990	June 1990– May 1991	June 1991 or later
Total	35.5	44.1	3.5	6.5	2.7	2.4	1.3	1.1	0.9	1.0	0.6	0.5
College expectations in sixth grade												
Decided to go	18.0	64.4	3.4	6.1	2.1	2.3	1.2	0.7	0.8	0.5	0.3	0.2
Planned not to go	54.4	24.6	3.3	6.4	2.6	2.6	1.4	1.4	0.9	1.0	0.9	0.6
Not sure	35.9	43.7	4.3	6.5	2.6	2.0	1.5	1.0	0.4	1.3	0.6	0.3
Hadn't thought about it	30.6	46.3	4.2	6.4	3.7	2.8	1.4	1.1	1.3	1.2	0.5	0.5
Postsecondary expectations in 1982												
None	75.7	4.7	1.8	4.5	2.5	3.0	1.5	1.6	1.3	1.5	1.0	0.9
Vocational/technical	43.6	27.1	5.5	8.7	4.2	3.6	1.8	1.6	1.6	1.1	0.7	0.5
Less-than-4-year degree	23.5	51.8	5.2	8.8	2.9	2.9	1.3	1.0	0.6	1.0	0.4	0.7
College degree	9.0	76.7	3.1	5.0	2.2	1.4	1.3	0.4	0.6	0.3	0.1	0.1
Advanced degree	7.3	80.4	2.5	5.5	1.5	1.2	0.4	0.4	0.2	0.4	0.2	0.0
First postsecondary institution type												
Never enrolled	100.0	0.0	0.0	0.0	0.0	0.0	0.0	0.0	0.0	0.0	0.0	0.0
Private for-profit	0.0	39.6	10.1	15.8	10.7	7.8	3.6	4.1	1.1	3.9	2.3	1.0
Private not-for-profit less-than-4-year	0.0	66.2	3.8	15.0	5.9	2.7	0.3	0.3	2.4	2.7	0.9	0.0
Public less-than-2-year	0.0	48.5	8.3	13.6	8.8	7.2	4.7	2.6	0.7	3.5	1.6	0.4
Public 2-year	0.0	58.6	7.7	12.5	4.5	5.2	2.4	2.2	2.5	1.8	1.3	1.2
Public 4-year	0.0	84.5	2.2	6.4	2.2	1.3	1.2	0.5	0.8	0.4	0.4	0.2
Private not-for-profit 4-year	0.0	86.9	2.3	5.3	1.7	1.2	0.9	0.7	0.3	0.2	0.1	0.5
Number of applications to college in 1982												
Did not apply	56.3	17.9	3.7	7.8	3.4	3.5	1.8	1.6	1.3	1.3	0.9	0.6
1 college	9.9	77.0	3.8	4.6	1.6	1.1	0.6	0.3	0.3	0.3	0.3	0.2
2–3 colleges	5.6	82.7	2.8	3.9	2.3	1.0	0.7	0.2	0.5	0.3	0.0	0.1
4 or more colleges	5.0	89.9	0.7	3.2	0.3	0.8	0.0	0.1	0.0	0.0	0.1	0.0

Table 2.2—Percentage distribution of 1980 high school sophomores by the timing of their first postsecondary enrollment, by selected characteristics—Continued

Student characteristics	Never enrolled	Before November 1982	November 1982– May 1983	June 1983– May 1984	June 1984– May 1985	June 1985– May 1986	June 1986– May 1987	June 1987– May 1988	June 1988– May 1989	June 1989– May 1990	June 1990– May 1991	June 1991 or later
Accepted at 1982 first choice college												
No applications	62.4	10.2	3.3	7.1	4.0	4.1	2.1	1.9	1.7	1.4	1.1	0.9
Attended first choice	0.0	89.7	3.8	5.0	0.8	0.3	0.2	0.1	0.0	0.1	0.1	0.0
Accepted but did not attend	23.3	51.0	5.3	8.2	4.3	2.3	1.8	1.2	1.0	0.9	0.4	0.3
Was not accepted at first choice	12.8	73.1	2.7	7.1	1.9	1.0	0.4	0.1	0.4	0.0	0.5	0.0

NOTES: Percentages may not sum to 100 percent due to rounding. The percentage of students in the "never enrolled" category does not match the percentages in other tables due to a different pattern of missing data in the variables used to specify the timing of first enrollment.

SOURCE: National Center for Education Statistics, High School & Beyond: 1980 Sophomore Cohort, 1980–1992.

Table 2.3—Percentage distribution of 1980 high school sophomores by the timing, intensity, and institution type of their initial enrollment in postsecondary education, by selected characteristics

Student characteristics	Fall 1982 full-time 4-year	Fall 1982 full-time public 2-year	Fall 1982 part-time 4-year	Fall 1982 part-time public 2-year	Fall 1982 other	Delay 4-year	Delay public 2-year	Delay other	Other enrollment	No enrollment
Total	23.4	10.5	1.1	4.1	5.0	4.2	10.3	5.9	1.9	33.6
Sex										
Male	22.0	9.3	1.0	3.4	4.3	4.7	10.3	5.0	1.9	38.1
Female	24.8	11.6	1.2	4.8	5.8	3.8	10.2	6.8	1.9	29.3
High school diploma status in 1982										
Regular diploma	28.2	12.2	1.3	4.6	5.8	4.5	10.1	5.3	1.6	26.3
Returned for diploma	1.9	6.1	0.8	4.9	3.0	3.8	17.6	11.3	1.7	48.7
Returned but no diploma	0.0	3.0	0.1	0.9	1.1	4.1	7.9	15.6	7.7	59.7
Never returned	1.0	1.3	0.0	0.4	0.9	1.5	7.3	6.5	2.7	78.4
Postsecondary expectations 1982										
None	0.7	1.3	0.1	1.2	1.4	2.9	10.5	6.3	2.6	73.1
Vocational/technical	1.9	9.1	0.5	4.1	11.6	3.9	14.0	11.5	2.4	41.1
Less-than-4-year degree	15.8	21.3	1.7	7.1	5.9	5.0	14.9	4.8	2.1	21.4
College degree	51.3	14.1	1.9	5.5	3.9	5.4	6.1	2.9	1.0	8.0
Advanced degree	60.1	11.0	1.8	3.8	3.7	5.0	5.1	2.2	0.7	6.6
Socioeconomic status (1980)										
Low quartile	8.7	7.9	0.6	2.3	4.3	4.0	9.3	8.3	2.7	52.0
Middle two quartiles	21.5	11.9	1.4	5.2	6.1	4.1	11.8	5.7	1.4	31.0
High quartile	48.4	12.3	1.3	4.9	5.1	5.4	6.6	3.0	1.4	11.7
Test score composite (1982)										
Low quartile	5.2	5.6	0.2	2.8	3.9	3.1	9.5	8.1	2.8	58.8
Middle two quartiles	17.7	13.6	1.4	5.1	6.2	4.4	11.9	6.4	1.8	31.6
High quartile	60.4	10.0	1.8	3.2	4.3	4.7	6.2	2.5	0.5	6.4
Race-ethnicity										
Native American/Alaska Native	8.4	6.1	0.2	2.8	3.0	9.2	16.6	5.2	2.5	46.0
Asian/Pacific Islander	40.6	16.1	2.1	7.0	2.8	3.7	11.1	3.3	0.8	12.5
Black	18.9	8.8	0.7	2.8	4.3	5.1	9.7	8.6	2.5	38.7
Hispanic	11.1	9.5	1.4	3.8	4.6	3.8	10.7	6.1	2.1	46.9
White	25.6	11.0	1.1	4.4	5.3	4.1	10.1	5.5	1.7	31.2

Table 2.3—Percentage distribution of 1980 high school sophomores by the timing, intensity, and institution type of their initial enrollment in postsecondary education, by selected characteristics—Continued

Student characteristics	Fall 1982 full-time 4-year	Fall 1982 full-time public 2-year	Fall 1982 part-time 4-year	Fall 1982 part-time public 2-year	Fall 1982 other	Delay 4-year	Delay public 2-year	Delay other	Other enrollment	No enrollment
Parents' educational attainment in 1980										
No high school diploma	12.9	9.8	1.0	3.3	5.3	3.8	11.6	7.2	2.2	42.9
High school graduate	18.9	8.1	0.7	4.3	5.7	3.7	16.0	8.4	1.5	32.7
Vocational/technical	22.9	12.5	1.3	4.5	6.2	3.9	11.5	7.4	2.2	27.7
Some college	35.5	14.1	1.3	6.2	4.8	5.5	9.2	4.3	1.1	18.1
Bachelor's degree	50.6	13.0	1.6	4.9	3.6	3.7	6.6	3.0	1.6	11.6
Advanced degree	52.9	7.5	1.0	3.3	5.7	7.2	6.8	2.8	0.9	12.0

NOTE: Percentages may not sum to 100 percent due to rounding.

SOURCE: National Center for Education Statistics, High School & Beyond: 1980 Sophomore Cohort, 1980–1992.

29

Table 2.4.A—Percentage distribution of 1980 high school sophomores by highest degree earned through 1992, by selected characteristics

Student characteristics	Less than high school	High school	Certificate	Associate's	Bachelor's	Master's	Professional	Doctorate
Total	5.8	51.5	11.0	7.9	20.0	2.7	0.9	0.2
Sex								
Male	6.5	53.5	9.7	6.7	19.5	2.6	1.3	0.2
Female	5.0	49.5	12.4	9.1	20.5	2.8	0.5	0.1
High school diploma status in 1982								
Regular diploma	0.3	51.9	10.8	8.7	23.9	3.2	1.1	0.2
Returned for diploma	6.8	68.3	14.4	7.0	3.4	0.1	0.1	0.0
Returned but no diploma	27.1	47.7	19.9	3.4	1.9	0.0	0.0	0.0
Never returned	51.5	35.7	9.5	2.1	0.9	0.3	0.0	0.0
Postsecondary expectations in 1982								
None	15.5	71.1	9.3	3.0	1.0	0.1	0.0	0.1
Vocational/technical	4.6	61.6	19.8	10.7	3.3	0.1	0.0	0.0
Less-than-4-year degree	1.6	53.2	13.3	15.6	15.0	1.1	0.2	0.0
College degree	0.9	35.3	6.8	6.3	44.9	5.0	0.8	0.1
Advanced degree	0.8	28.9	5.2	5.7	45.1	9.0	4.4	0.8
Socioeconomic status (1980)								
Low quartile	9.0	64.6	12.3	6.9	6.4	0.7	0.1	0.0
Middle two quartiles	3.9	53.8	11.5	9.1	19.0	2.0	0.5	0.1
High quartile	1.4	32.7	7.0	7.6	41.2	6.9	2.7	0.5
Test score composite (1982)								
Low quartile	15.6	64.0	13.0	4.1	3.0	0.2	0.0	0.1
Middle two quartiles	3.1	56.2	12.8	10.1	16.1	1.5	0.3	0.0
High quartile	0.1	26.5	4.8	7.2	49.2	8.7	3.0	0.6
Type of start in postsecondary education								
Fall 1982 full-time 4-year	0.0	21.2	3.5	4.6	57.8	9.0	3.4	0.5
Fall 1982 full-time public 2-year	0.3	36.5	11.9	24.4	24.6	2.1	0.2	0.0
Fall 1982 part-time 4-year	0.0	52.2	6.7	10.0	27.2	3.5	0.1	0.4
Fall 1982 part-time public 2-year	1.6	59.5	13.4	9.4	14.4	0.9	0.8	0.0
Fall 1982 other	0.2	23.0	34.3	24.5	15.7	1.9	0.4	0.0
Delay 4-year	0.4	55.6	8.1	7.4	24.0	3.7	0.4	0.4
Delay public 2-year	1.7	63.0	16.9	12.0	6.2	0.2	0.0	0.0
Delay other	1.9	31.4	48.4	14.4	3.8	0.1	0.1	0.0
Other enrollment	0.0	0.0	86.5	5.1	6.0	1.1	0.4	0.8
No enrollment	16.1	83.9	0.0	0.0	0.0	0.0	0.0	0.0

Table 2.4.A—Percentage distribution of 1980 high school sophomores by highest degree earned through 1992, by selected characteristics—Continued

Student characteristics	Less than high school	High school	Certificate	Associate's	Bachelor's	Master's	Professional	Doctorate
Race–ethnicity								
Native American/Alaska Native	17.8	58.2	11.8	5.0	6.7	0.5	0.0	0.0
Asian/Pacific Islander	0.6	40.9	6.9	6.2	32.7	4.7	7.5	0.7
Black	6.9	59.6	16.3	5.2	10.0	1.5	0.5	0.2
Hispanic	11.9	59.6	11.2	7.3	9.0	0.6	0.3	0.0
White	4.9	49.1	10.1	8.4	23.1	3.2	1.0	0.2
Parents' educational attainment in 1980								
No high school diploma	6.5	59.8	12.8	8.6	10.8	1.2	0.3	0.1
High school graduate	5.2	59.1	12.4	6.0	16.6	0.3	0.4	0.0
Vocational/technical	3.0	49.2	15.4	10.2	19.1	2.4	0.5	0.1
Some college	2.1	43.7	8.4	8.4	32.0	4.3	1.0	0.2
Bachelor's degree	1.4	32.6	4.9	8.1	42.4	6.9	3.1	0.5
Advanced degree	3.5	23.9	8.6	4.9	44.1	10.0	4.3	0.7

NOTE: Percentages may not sum to 100 percent due to rounding.

SOURCE: National Center for Education Statistics, High School & Beyond: 1980 Sophomore Cohort, 1980–1992.

31

Table 2.4.B—Percentage distribution of 1980 high school sophomores who enrolled in postsecondary education immediately after high school by highest degree attained through 1992, by selected characteristics

Student characteristics	High school	Certificate	Associate's	Bachelor's	Advanced degree
Total	29.6	10.0	12.2	40.3	7.9
Sex					
Male	29.5	8.6	10.1	42.3	9.5
Female	29.7	11.1	13.9	38.7	6.7
High school diploma status in 1982					
Regular diploma	29.0	9.6	11.9	41.3	8.2
Returned for diploma	51.0	20.4	20.3	7.6	0.7
Returned but no diploma	—	—	—	—	—
Never returned	45.0	25.4	13.1	16.5	0.0
Postsecondary expectations in 1982					
None	49.0	29.1	15.3	6.5	0.0
Vocational/technical	39.2	29.9	23.5	7.1	0.3
Less-than-4-year degree	36.7	13.3	23.9	23.9	2.2
College degree	26.6	5.2	6.6	54.3	7.4
Advanced degree	22.3	3.6	5.4	52.0	16.7
Socioeconomic status (1980)					
Low quartile	38.5	18.1	18.2	22.0	3.2
Middle two quartiles	33.2	11.0	14.1	36.4	5.4
High quartile	21.9	5.0	7.6	52.5	13.1
Test score composite (1982)					
Low quartile	48.5	23.4	13.7	13.3	1.1
Middle two quartiles	35.5	12.5	16.1	32.1	3.9
High quartile	17.9	2.9	7.1	57.2	14.9
Race–ethnicity					
Native American/Alaska Native	38.0	23.1	10.1	26.3	2.6
Asian/Pacific Islander	23.6	5.9	6.5	45.3	18.6
Black	43.8	19.4	8.6	23.3	4.9
Hispanic-Mexican	43.1	11.4	16.0	26.5	2.9
White	27.0	8.7	12.4	43.5	8.5
Parents' educational attainment in 1980					
No high school diploma	35.5	13.3	18.1	28.6	4.4
High school graduate	36.1	13.9	7.5	40.9	1.6
Vocational/technical	30.3	12.0	14.4	37.0	6.3
Some college	27.8	7.5	9.8	46.5	8.4
Bachelor's degree	22.2	2.7	8.5	53.7	12.9
Advanced degree	15.4	6.8	5.2	53.0	19.6

—Sample size is too small for a reliable estimate.

NOTES: Students who enrolled in postsecondary education before November 1982 were defined as immediate entrants. Percentages may not sum to 100 percent due to rounding.

SOURCE: National Center for Education Statistics, High School & Beyond: 1980 Sophomore Cohort, 1980–1992.

Table 2.4.C—Percentage distribution of 1980 high school sophomores who delayed entry into postsecondary education by highest degree attained through 1992, by selected characteristics

Student characteristics	High school	Certificate	Associate's	Bachelor's	Advanced degree
Total	53.8	24.2	11.8	9.2	1.1
Sex					
Male	53.1	22.7	12.4	10.8	1.0
Female	54.4	25.6	11.2	7.7	1.2
High school diploma status in 1982					
Regular diploma	54.2	22.4	12.0	10.5	0.9
Diploma returned	54.8	28.3	10.8	5.8	0.3
Returned no diploma	42.9	40.8	9.3	7.0	0.0
Had not returned	51.9	35.7	9.5	1.2	1.7
Postsecondary expectations in 1982					
None	57.9	27.4	11.2	3.0	0.6
Vocational/technical	50.3	32.0	13.8	3.9	0.0
Less-than-4-year degree	57.9	18.5	12.4	10.5	0.8
College degree	54.6	15.5	8.8	20.0	1.2
Advanced degree	43.7	16.6	10.3	23.8	5.6
Socioeconomic status (1980)					
Low quartile	57.3	25.8	11.5	5.3	0.1
Middle two quartiles	54.4	24.5	11.8	8.7	0.7
High quartile	45.5	16.7	14.3	19.9	3.7
Test score composite (1982)					
Low quartile	61.0	28.4	7.8	2.8	0.0
Middle two quartiles	53.2	25.7	12.7	7.9	0.6
High quartile	44.6	17.2	10.7	24.5	3.0
Race–ethnicity					
Native American/Alaska Native	72.2	15.0	8.8	4.0	0.0
Asian/Pacific Islander	72.1	11.5	9.2	7.3	0.0
Black	54.8	29.7	8.3	6.6	0.6
Hispanic	57.6	27.9	10.4	3.9	0.2
White	52.6	23.1	12.3	10.7	1.4
Parents' educational attainment in 1980					
No high school diploma	54.3	28.0	11.3	6.0	0.3
High school graduate	64.1	20.5	11.0	4.4	0.0
Vocational/technical	46.8	33.1	14.0	5.8	0.4
Some college	56.4	15.6	11.9	15.1	1.0
Bachelor's degree	46.1	15.2	14.3	17.3	7.1
Advanced degree	29.7	19.9	7.4	35.9	7.1

NOTES: Percentages may not sum to 100 percent due to rounding. Students who enrolled in postsecondary education after November 1982 were defined as delayed entrants.

SOURCE: National Center for Education Statistics, High School & Beyond: 1980 Sophomore Cohort, 1980–1992.

Table 2.5—Average length of initial delay in months prior to entry into postsecondary education among 1980 high school sophomores, by highest degree attained through 1992 and selected characteristics

	High school	Certificate	Associate's	Bachelor's	Advanced degree	Average, all degrees
Total	19.0	22.8	12.5	5.6	5.0	14.0
Sex						
Male	20.2	25.6	13.8	6.2	4.8	14.9
Female	18.0	20.7	11.6	5.0	5.2	13.3
High school diploma status in 1982						
Regular diploma	17.9	21.3	11.3	5.5	4.8	12.9
Diploma returned	30.3	37.8	29.4	—	—	30.9
Returned no diploma	—	—	—	—	—	21.9
Had not returned	24.2	32.9	—	—	—	26.2
Postsecondary expectations in 1982						
None	38.4	39.2	32.2	—	—	37.6
Vocational/technical	22.5	23.1	14.4	11.9	—	20.6
Less-than-4-year degree	17.4	16.1	8.2	6.7	5.9	13.2
College degree	12.1	17.6	9.0	4.7	4.4	8.2
Advanced degree	9.6	8.7	10.7	5.1	4.9	6.7
Type of start in postsecondary education						
Full-time fall 1982 4-year	4.0	3.9	4.0	4.0	3.9	4.0
Full-time fall 1982 public 2-year	4.0	4.5	4.0	3.9	3.4	4.0
Part-time fall 1982 4-year	4.6	—	—	3.5	—	4.1
Part-time fall 1982 public 2-year	4.1	13.7	4.2	3.9	—	5.2
Delay 4-year	33.3	28.9	29.5	19.4	—	28.9
Delay public 2-year	36.6	30.8	30.6	20.6	—	33.9
Fall 1982 other	4.0	3.8	3.6	4.2	—	3.9
Delay other	25.4	35.0	32.9	—	—	30.9
Other	—	44.2	—	—	—	41.0
Socioeconomic status						
Low quartile	23.8	29.2	15.2	7.8	—	21.5
Middle two quartiles	19.9	20.2	11.6	5.7	4.5	14.4
High quartile	11.9	15.2	9.5	4.9	4.9	7.9
Test score composite in 1982						
Low quartile	24.7	31.5	17.1	8.3	—	24.6
Middle two quartiles	17.9	19.8	11.3	6.1	4.9	14.2
High quartile	12.7	16.7	7.7	4.9	4.3	7.3
Race–ethnicity						
Native American/Alaska Native	31.2	23.0	—	—	—	25.7
Asian/Pacific Islander	11.9	—	—	4.3	3.8	8.3
Black	20.7	20.8	14.1	6.3	7.6	17.4
Hispanic	20.1	28.2	13.0	5.8	4.1	17.8
White	18.5	22.9	11.8	5.5	4.9	13.1
Parents educational attainment by 1980						
No high school diploma	22.4	28.3	13.3	6.4	4.4	18.9
High school graduate	22.3	23.5	16.3	5.4	—	17.8
Vocational/technical	19.7	20.4	12.0	5.1	4.2	14.2
Some college	15.0	15.5	12.3	5.4	4.6	10.3
Bachelor's degree	9.1	18.7	6.9	4.8	5.3	7.0
Advanced degree	10.9	16.7	6.3	5.8	5.1	7.6

—Sample size is too small for a reliable estimate.

SOURCE: National Center for Education Statistics High School & Beyond: 1980 Sophomore Cohort, 1980–1992.

Table 2.6.A—Percentage of 1980 high school sophomores attaining degrees and average number of months between first enrollment and attainment of degrees, by type of degree and selected characteristics

Student characteristics	Percentage who attained certificate	Average months to certificate	Percentage who attained associate's	Average months to associate's	Percentage who attained bachelor's	Average months to bachelor's
Total	12.1	29.7	9.4	36.8	22.4	55.7
Sex						
Male	10.3	30.3	8.2	37.7	22.2	56.4
Female	13.8	29.3	10.6	36.1	22.6	55.1
Postsecondary expectations in 1982						
None	8.5	18.6	3.1	30.8	0.9	—
Vocational/technical	20.3	20.0	10.6	30.0	3.0	61.0
Less-than-4-year degree	14.4	36.4	17.4	36.3	15.4	61.6
College degree	8.9	44.2	10.2	39.8	48.9	55.8
Advanced degree	7.8	44.8	8.8	43.6	56.9	53.6
Type of start in postsecondary education						
Full-time fall 1982 4-year	6.4	57.2	6.0	47.0	68.6	53.1
Full-time fall 1982 public 2-year	15.0	43.4	34.4	34.6	25.5	66.5
Part-time fall 1982 4-year	8.8	—	11.8	—	30.7	71.2
Part-time fall 1982 public 2-year	14.6	37.7	9.6	55.7	14.9	67.7
Delay 4-year	9.7	36.5	7.2	41.1	26.4	49.0
Delay public 2-year	18.1	32.6	13.1	38.1	5.8	66.9
Fall 1982 other	35.5	19.5	27.0	27.8	16.9	58.5
Delay other	47.9	16.5	14.8	28.7	3.9	—
Other	85.0	15.1	5.0	—	5.6	—
Socioeconomic status (1980)						
Low quartile	12.8	23.9	7.0	36.9	6.6	55.9
Middle two quartiles	12.5	29.9	11.2	34.9	20.3	56.8
High quartile	9.3	38.0	10.4	38.9	49.2	54.4
Test score composite (1982)						
Low quartile	13.0	24.1	4.0	29.8	2.8	62.8
Middle two quartiles	14.1	29.3	12.0	35.9	17.1	57.9
High quartile	6.8	45.8	10.0	39.9	59.0	53.6
Race–ethnicity						
Native American/Alaska Native	12.2	33.0	5.2	—	6.4	—
Asian/Pacific Islander	7.4	—	8.1	40.5	42.5	59.0
Black	17.0	31.5	5.2	40.2	11.1	57.3
Hispanic	12.2	28.7	7.9	45.3	9.3	60.0
White	11.1	29.5	10.4	35.3	25.9	55.3
Parents' educational attainment in 1980						
No high school diploma	12.8	24.3	9.3	33.0	11.2	57.2
High school graduate	12.7	29.3	6.6	36.2	16.4	53.1
Vocational/technical	16.6	29.6	12.1	34.7	21.5	57.8
Some college	10.3	34.0	11.6	42.0	35.5	56.1
Bachelor's degree	7.0	45.5	11.7	36.4	50.5	54.9
Advanced degree	11.5	46.9	6.0	35.5	57.3	52.5

—Sample size is too small for a reliable estimate.

NOTE: The percentage of students at each attainment level does not necessarily match the percentage distributions by highest degree because students can have earned degrees other than their highest degree.

SOURCE: National Center for Education Statistics, High School & Beyond: 1980 Sophomore Cohort, 1980–1992.

Table 2.6.B—Percentage of 1980 high school sophomores who entered postsecondary education before November 1982 attaining degrees and average number of months between first enrollment and attainment of degrees, by type of degree and selected characteristics

Student characteristics	Percentage who attained certificate	Average months to certificate	Percentage who attained associate's	Average months to associate's	Percentage who attained bachelor's	Average months to bachelor's
Total	12.6	38.9	15.6	37.4	46.5	55.8
Sex						
Male	10.5	42.9	13.7	38.1	50.0	56.7
Female	14.2	36.4	17.2	36.9	43.6	55.0
Postsecondary expectations in 1982						
None	28.1	28.0	15.6	—	6.1	—
Vocational/technical	33.4	23.6	24.3	28.3	7.0	68.3
Less-than-4-year degree	15.2	41.2	27.1	36.7	24.8	62.1
College degree	7.8	50.2	11.3	40.4	59.8	55.5
Advanced degree	6.4	54.6	9.1	44.1	66.5	53.9
Type of start in postsecondary education						
Full-time fall 1982 4-year	6.4	57.2	6.0	47.0	68.6	53.1
Full-time fall 1982 public 2-year	15.0	43.4	34.4	34.6	25.5	66.5
Part-time fall 1982 4-year	8.8	—	11.8	—	30.7	71.2
Part-time fall 1982 public 2-year	14.6	37.7	9.6	55.7	14.9	67.7
Fall 1982 other	35.5	19.5	27.0	27.8	16.9	58.5
Socioeconomic status (1980)						
Low quartile	20.6	34.0	18.6	36.8	23.9	57.0
Middle two quartiles	13.1	38.5	18.6	35.3	40.0	56.8
High quartile	8.2	44.9	11.2	40.8	63.5	54.7
Test score composite (1982)						
Low quartile	26.3	32.8	14.1	30.1	13.2	63.9
Middle two quartiles	15.6	37.1	20.4	36.6	34.8	58.5
High quartile	5.2	52.3	10.4	40.2	69.8	53.5
Race–ethnicity						
Native American/Alaska Native	24.3	—	15.0	—	25.9	—
Asian/Pacific Islander	7.2	—	8.8	38.3	60.7	58.2
Black	22.1	42.7	9.0	43.2	26.9	59.0
Hispanic	15.9	41.6	18.0	46.1	28.5	60.4
White	11.1	38.1	16.5	36.2	50.1	55.3
Parents' educational attainment by 1980						
No high school diploma	15.3	33.7	20.5	34.0	30.8	57.6
High school graduate	15.0	36.8	9.6	33.0	41.0	53.3
Vocational/technical	14.9	38.2	19.0	34.5	42.5	57.9
Some college	10.4	42.6	14.6	43.0	52.9	56.1
Bachelor's degree	5.7	55.3	12.9	38.4	64.4	54.8
Advanced degree	9.1	47.7	5.8	36.1	71.0	52.2

—Sample size is too small for a reliable estimate.

NOTE: The percentage of students at each attainment level does not necessarily match the percentage distributions by highest degree because students can have earned degrees other than their highest degree.

SOURCE: National Center for Education Statistics, High School & Beyond: 1980 Sophomore Cohort, 1980–1992.

Table 2.6.C—Percentage of 1980 high school sophomores who entered postsecondary education after October 1982 attaining degrees and average number of months between first enrollment and attainment of degrees, by type of degree and selected characteristics

Student characteristics	Percentage who attained certificate	Average months to certificate	Percentage who attained associate's	Average months to associate's	Percentage who attained bachelor's	Average months to bachelor's
Total	25.0	24.0	12.4	35.2	9.5	54.3
Sex						
Male	23.5	22.9	13.3	37.1	11.0	52.3
Female	26.4	24.9	11.5	33.1	8.0	56.9
Postsecondary expectations 1982						
None	25.9	17.5	11.9	29.1	2.6	—
Vocational/technical	31.8	18.4	13.5	32.8	3.9	—
Less-than-4-year degree	20.5	36.2	13.3	34.1	10.7	59.7
College degree	16.5	35.6	10.6	37.2	20.1	59.2
Advanced degree	19.4	24.8	11.2	41.4	27.6	48.2
Type of start in postsecondary education						
Delay 4-year	9.7	36.5	7.2	41.1	26.4	49.0
Delay public 2-year	18.1	32.6	13.1	38.1	5.8	66.9
Delay other	47.9	16.5	14.8	28.7	3.9	—
Socioeconomic status (1980)						
Low quartile	26.8	19.6	12.2	36.4	4.9	49.7
Middle two quartiles	24.6	23.1	11.9	33.7	8.6	56.5
High quartile	17.2	28.3	15.4	32.2	21.9	50.9
Test score composite (1982)						
Low quartile	28.6	22.1	7.3	29.4	2.4	—
Middle two quartiles	26.3	22.9	13.3	33.9	8.0	53.4
High quartile	18.8	36.3	12.7	38.3	25.1	55.8
Race–ethnicity						
Native American/Alaska Native	15.7	—	6.7	—	3.4	—
Asian/Pacific Islander	11.5	—	11.5	—	7.3	—
Black	30.7	25.1	8.1	36.4	6.9	47.8
Hispanic	27.2	23.8	10.6	41.7	3.1	55.9
White	23.6	23.0	13.2	32.5	11.1	54.6
Parents' educational attainment 1980						
No high school diploma	27.1	19.7	11.9	30.8	5.9	53.4
High school graduate	20.1	22.0	10.7	—	4.4	—
Vocational/technical	34.5	24.7	13.3	35.6	5.9	57.0
Some college	16.2	21.9	13.4	38.9	14.5	54.5
Bachelor's degree	15.7	—	15.8	—	21.0	53.3
Advanced degree	27.8	—	11.6	—	41.7	55.7

—Sample size is too small for a reliable estimate.

NOTE: The percentage of students at each attainment level does not necessarily match the percentage distributions by highest degree because students can have earned degrees other than their highest degree.

SOURCE: National Center for Education Statistics, High School & Beyond: 1980 Sophomore Cohort, 1980–1992.

Table 2.7.A—Average number of postsecondary institutions attended prior to degree attainment by 1980 high school sophomores, by type of degree and selected characteristics

Student characteristics	Certificate	Associate's	Bachelor's
Total	1.5	1.5	1.7
Sex			
Male	1.5	1.5	1.7
Female	1.5	1.5	1.8
Postsecondary expectations 1982			
None	1.2	1.2	1.8
Vocational/technical	1.2	1.3	1.9
Less-than-4-year degree	1.6	1.4	1.9
College degree	2.0	1.7	1.7
Advanced degree	2.1	1.7	1.7
Type of start in postsecondary education			
Full-time fall 1982 4-year	2.4	2.1	1.6
Full-time fall 1982 public 2-year	1.8	1.3	2.3
Part-time fall 1982 4-year	—	—	2.3
Part-time fall 1982 public 2-year	1.8	1.6	2.5
Delay 4-year	1.9	1.6	1.5
Delay public 2-year	1.6	1.4	2.3
Fall 1982 other	1.2	1.4	2.1
Delay other	1.2	1.3	—
Other	1.1	—	—
Socioeconomic status (1980)			
Low quartile	1.3	1.4	1.6
Middle two quartiles	1.5	1.4	1.7
High quartile	1.8	1.6	1.8
Test score composite (1982)			
Low quartile	1.4	1.3	1.7
Middle two quartiles	1.5	1.4	1.8
High quartile	1.9	1.7	1.7
Race–ethnicity			
Native American/Alaska Native	1.4	—	—
Asian/Pacific Islander	1.6	1.7	1.9
Black	1.6	1.5	1.6
Hispanic	1.6	1.6	1.8
White	1.5	1.5	1.8
Parents' educational attainment 1980			
No high school diploma	1.4	1.3	1.7
High school graduate	1.5	1.1	1.6
Vocational/technical	1.5	1.5	1.8
Some college	1.7	1.6	1.8
Bachelor's degree	2.0	1.6	1.9
Advanced degree	1.9	1.6	1.7

—Sample size is too small for a reliable estimate.

SOURCE: National Center for Education Statistics, High School & Beyond: 1980 Sophomore Cohort, 1980–1992.

Table 2.7.B—Average number of postsecondary institutions attended prior to degree attainment by 1980 high school sophomores who first enrolled before November 1982, by type of degree and selected characteristics

Student characteristics	Certificate	Associate's	Bachelor's
Total	1.7	1.5	1.7
Sex			
Male	1.7	1.6	1.7
Female	1.7	1.5	1.8
Postsecondary expectations 1982			
None	1.3	—	—
Vocational/technical	1.3	1.3	2.0
Less-than-4-year degree	1.7	1.5	1.9
College degree	2.2	1.7	1.7
Advanced degree	2.4	1.7	1.8
Type of start in postsecondary education			
Full-time fall 1982 4-year	2.4	2.1	1.6
Full-time fall 1982 public 2-year	1.8	1.3	2.3
Part-time fall 1982 4-year	—	—	2.3
Part-time fall 1982 public 2-year	1.8	1.6	2.5
Fall 1982 other	1.2	1.4	2.1
Socioeconomic status (1980)			
Low quartile	1.5	1.5	1.6
Middle two quartiles	1.6	1.5	1.7
High quartile	2.1	1.7	1.8
Test score composite (1982)			
Low quartile	1.5	1.4	1.7
Middle two quartiles	1.7	1.5	1.8
High quartile	2.1	1.7	1.7
Race–ethnicity			
Native American/Alaska Native	—	—	—
Asian/Pacific Islander	—	1.7	1.9
Black	1.8	1.6	1.6
Hispanic	2.0	1.7	1.8
White	1.7	1.5	1.7
Parents' educational attainment 1980			
No high school diploma	1.6	1.4	1.7
High school graduate	1.7	1.2	1.5
Vocational/technical	1.7	1.5	1.8
Some college	1.9	1.7	1.8
Bachelor's degree	2.4	1.7	1.9
Advanced degree	2.0	1.6	1.7

—Sample size is too small for a reliable estimate.

SOURCE: National Center for Education Statistics, High School & Beyond: 1980 Sophomore Cohort, 1980–1992.

Table 2.7.C—Average number of postsecondary institutions attended prior to degree attainment by 1980 high school sophomores who first enrolled after October 1982, by type of degree and selected characteristics

Student characteristics	Certificate	Associate's	Bachelor's
Total	1.4	1.4	1.8
Sex			
Male	1.4	1.4	1.8
Female	1.4	1.4	1.8
Postsecondary expectations in 1982			
None	1.2	1.2	—
Vocational/technical	1.2	1.3	—
Less-than-4-year degree	1.7	1.3	1.8
College degree	1.7	1.7	2.1
Advanced degree	1.6	1.6	1.6
Type of start in postsecondary education			
Delay 4-year	1.9	1.6	1.5
Delay public 2-year	1.6	1.4	2.3
Delay other	1.2	1.3	—
Socioeconomic status (1980)			
Low quartile	1.3	1.4	1.8
Middle two quartiles	1.4	1.3	1.9
High quartile	1.5	1.5	1.6
Test score composite (1982)			
Low quartile	1.3	1.3	—
Middle two quartiles	1.4	1.3	1.7
High quartile	1.6	1.5	1.9
Race–ethnicity			
Native American/Alaska Native	—	—	—
Asian/Pacific Islander	—	—	—
Black	1.6	1.5	1.7
Hispanic	1.5	1.4	2.0
White	1.3	1.3	1.8
Parents' educational attainment in 1980			
No high school diploma	1.4	1.2	1.7
High school graduate	1.3	—	—
Vocational/technical	1.4	1.4	1.9
Some college	1.5	1.5	1.7
Bachelor's degree	1.6	—	1.7
Advanced degree	—	—	1.8

—Sample size is too small for a reliable estimate.

SOURCE: National Center for Education Statistics, High School & Beyond: 1980 Sophomore Cohort, 1980–1992.

Table 2.7.D—Percentage distribution of 1980 high school sophomores who first enrolled before November 1982, by average number of postsecondary institutions attended prior to bachelor's degree attainment and selected characteristics

Student characteristics	One	Two	Three or more
Total	50.4	31.8	17.8
Sex			
Male	50.5	32.3	17.2
Female	50.3	31.4	18.3
Postsecondary expectations in 1982			
None	—	—	—
Vocational/technical	33.2	34.0	32.8
Less-than-4-year degree	40.0	37.3	22.7
College degree	53.4	31.1	15.5
Advanced degree	50.5	31.3	18.2
Type of start in postsecondary education			
Full-time fall 1982 4-year	60.8	25.0	14.2
Full-time fall 1982 public 2-year	7.9	62.0	30.2
Part-time fall 1982 4-year	37.5	27.4	35.1
Part-time fall 1982 public 2-year	7.8	54.6	37.6
Fall 1982 other	26.5	49.7	23.8
Socioeconomic status (1980)			
Low quartile	55.3	34.3	10.4
Middle two quartiles	52.3	31.0	16.7
High quartile	47.8	33.8	18.4
Test score composite (1982)			
Low quartile	48.9	37.0	14.1
Middle two quartiles	44.2	34.4	21.4
High quartile	54.4	30.2	15.5
Race–ethnicity			
Native American/Alaska Native	—	—	—
Asian/Pacific Islander	37.9	40.4	21.7
Black	58.4	29.1	12.6
Hispanic	51.5	28.8	19.7
White	50.1	31.9	18.0
Parents' educational attainment in 1980			
No high school diploma	53.7	30.0	16.3
High school graduate	59.4	30.6	10.0
Vocational/technical	48.2	31.8	19.9
Some college	47.3	34.9	17.9
Bachelor's degree	46.6	30.8	22.7
Advanced degree	56.4	28.7	15.0

—Sample size is too small for a reliable estimate.

NOTE: Percentages may not sum to 100 percent due to rounding.

SOURCE: National Center for Education Statistics, High School & Beyond: 1980 Sophomore Cohort, 1980–1992.

Table 2.8.A—Average number of periods of enrollment prior to degree attainment among 1980 high school sophomores, by type of degree and selected characteristics

Student characteristics	Certificate	Associate's	Bachelor's
Total	1.3	1.3	1.2
Sex			
Male	1.3	1.3	1.3
Female	1.3	1.2	1.2
Postsecondary expectations in 1982			
None	1.2	1.2	1.2
Vocational/technical	1.2	1.2	1.6
Less-than-4-year degree	1.4	1.2	1.4
College degree	1.6	1.3	1.2
Advanced degree	1.5	1.3	1.2
Type of start in postsecondary education			
Full-time fall 1982 4-year	1.8	1.5	1.2
Full-time fall 1982 public 2-year	1.5	1.2	1.5
Part-time fall 1982 4-year	—	—	1.5
Part-time fall 1982 public 2-year	1.4	1.4	1.4
Delay 4-year	1.6	1.4	1.2
Delay public 2-year	1.5	1.3	1.6
Fall 1982 other	1.1	1.2	1.4
Delay other	1.1	1.2	—
Other	1.0	—	—
Socioeconomic status (1980)			
Low quartile	1.2	1.2	1.2
Middle two quartiles	1.3	1.2	1.3
High quartile	1.5	1.3	1.2
Test score composite (1982)			
Low quartile	1.3	1.2	1.3
Middle two quartiles	1.3	1.2	1.3
High quartile	1.5	1.3	1.2
Race–ethnicity			
Native American/Alaska Native	1.3	—	—
Asian/Pacific Islander	1.4	1.2	1.3
Black	1.4	1.3	1.2
Hispanic	1.3	1.3	1.3
White	1.3	1.2	1.3
Parents' educational attainment in 1980			
No high school diploma	1.3	1.2	1.3
High school graduate	1.3	1.1	1.2
Vocational/technical	1.3	1.2	1.2
Some college	1.3	1.3	1.3
Bachelor's degree	1.6	1.3	1.2
Advanced degree	1.6	1.4	1.2

—Sample size is too small for a reliable estimate.

SOURCE: National Center for Education Statistics, High School & Beyond: 1980 Sophomore Cohort, 1980–1992.

Table 2.8.B—Average number of periods of enrollment prior to degree attainment among 1980 high school sophomores who first enrolled before November 1982, by type of degree and selected characteristics

Student characteristics	Certificate	Associate's	Bachelor's
Total	1.4	1.3	1.2
Sex			
Male	1.4	1.3	1.2
Female	1.4	1.2	1.2
Postsecondary expectations in 1982			
None	1.3	—	—
Vocational/technical	1.2	1.2	1.7
Less-than-4-year degree	1.4	1.2	1.3
College degree	1.6	1.3	1.2
Advanced degree	1.6	1.3	1.2
Type of start in postsecondary education			
Full-time fall 1982 4-year	1.8	1.5	1.2
Full-time fall 1982 public 2-year	1.5	1.2	1.5
Part-time fall 1982 4-year	—	—	1.5
Part-time fall 1982 public 2-year	1.4	1.4	1.4
Fall 1982 other	1.1	1.2	1.4
Socioeconomic status (1980)			
Low quartile	1.3	1.3	1.2
Middle two quartiles	1.4	1.2	1.2
High quartile	1.6	1.3	1.2
Test score composite (1982)			
Low quartile	1.4	1.2	1.2
Middle two quartiles	1.4	1.2	1.3
High quartile	1.6	1.3	1.2
Race–ethnicity			
Native American/Alaska Native	—	—	—
Asian/Pacific Islander	—	1.2	1.3
Black	1.6	1.4	1.2
Hispanic	1.4	1.3	1.3
White	1.4	1.2	1.2
Parents' educational attainment in 1980			
No high school diploma	1.3	1.2	1.3
High school graduate	1.4	1.1	1.1
Vocational/technical	1.3	1.2	1.2
Some college	1.5	1.3	1.3
Bachelor's degree	1.9	1.3	1.2
Advanced degree	1.5	1.3	1.2

—Sample size is too small for a reliable estimate.

SOURCE: National Center for Education Statistics, High School & Beyond: 1980 Sophomore Cohort, 1980–1992.

Table 2.8.C—Average number of periods of enrollment prior to degree attainment among 1980 high school sophomores who first enrolled after October 1982, by type of degree and selected characteristics

Student characteristics	Certificate	Associate's	Bachelor's
Total	1.3	1.3	1.4
Sex			
Male	1.3	1.3	1.4
Female	1.3	1.2	1.4
Postsecondary expectations in 1982			
None	1.2	1.2	—
Vocational/technical	1.2	1.2	—
Less-than-4-year degree	1.5	1.2	1.4
College degree	1.6	1.3	1.4
Advanced degree	1.4	1.3	1.3
Type of start in postsecondary education			
Delay 4-year	1.6	1.4	1.2
Delay public 2-year	1.5	1.3	1.6
Delay other	1.1	1.2	—
Socioeconomic status (1980)			
Low quartile	1.2	1.2	1.3
Middle two quartiles	1.3	1.2	1.4
High quartile	1.3	1.3	1.3
Test score composite (1982)			
Low quartile	1.3	1.1	—
Middle two quartiles	1.3	1.2	1.2
High quartile	1.5	1.2	1.5
Race–ethnicity			
Native American/Alaska Native	—	—	—
Asian/Pacific Islander	—	—	—
Black	1.4	1.3	1.3
Hispanic	1.3	1.4	1.3
White	1.3	1.2	1.4
Parents' educational attainment in 1980			
No high school diploma	1.3	1.1	1.3
High school graduate	1.2	—	—
Vocational/technical	1.3	1.3	1.4
Some college	1.2	1.3	1.4
Bachelor's degree	1.3	—	1.2
Advanced degree	—	—	1.5

—Sample size is too small for a reliable estimate.

SOURCE: National Center for Education Statistics, High School & Beyond: 1980 Sophomore Cohort, 1980–1992.

Table 2.8.D—Percentage distribution of 1980 high school sophomores who first enrolled before November 1982, by average number of periods of enrollment prior to bachelor's degree attainment and selected characteristics

Student characteristics	One	Two	Three or more
Total	80.7	15.9	3.5
Sex			
Male	80.0	16.8	3.2
Female	81.3	15.1	3.7
Postsecondary expectations in 1982			
None	—	—	—
Vocational/technical	55.0	26.8	18.2
Less-than-4-year degree	70.5	24.5	5.0
College degree	81.8	14.1	4.0
Advanced degree	82.9	15.3	1.9
Type of start in postsecondary education			
Full-time fall 1982 4-year	85.2	12.6	2.3
Full-time fall 1982 public 2-year	63.6	29.0	7.4
Part-time fall 1982 4-year	63.4	27.2	9.5
Part-time fall 1982 public 2-year	67.7	23.3	9.1
Fall 1982 other	67.0	26.2	6.8
Socioeconomic status (1980)			
Low quartile	81.3	17.3	1.4
Middle two quartiles	80.4	16.1	3.5
High quartile	81.6	14.6	3.7
Test score composite (1982)			
Low quartile	81.2	16.2	2.6
Middle two quartiles	76.5	19.6	4.0
High quartile	83.0	14.1	2.9
Race–ethnicity			
Native American/Alaska Native	—	—	—
Asian/Pacific Islander	72.9	26.9	0.2
Black	84.3	13.4	2.3
Hispanic	75.7	21.2	3.1
White	80.7	15.6	3.7
Parents' educational attainment in 1980			
No high school diploma	78.9	17.1	4.0
High school graduate	88.0	12.0	0.1
Vocational/technical	79.4	18.2	2.4
Some college	79.3	16.3	4.5
Bachelor's degree	79.6	17.3	3.2
Advanced degree	85.9	11.3	2.9

—Sample size is too small for a reliable estimate.

NOTE: Percentages may not sum to 100 percent due to rounding.

SOURCE: National Center for Education Statistics, High School & Beyond: 1980 Sophomore Cohort, 1980–1992.

Table 2.9—Application to and acceptance by graduate and first professional programs among 1980 high school sophomores who had earned a bachelor's degree by 1992, by selected characteristics

Student characteristics	Took graduate/professional admission exams (%)	Applied to graduate or professional institution (%)	Accepted at first choice (%)	Number of applications
Total	68.1	30.8	82.4	2.6
Sex				
Male	66.9	30.8	77.9	2.9
Female	69.3	30.8	86.8	2.4
Postsecondary expectations in 1982				
None	77.3	25.9	—	—
Vocational/technical	91.7	16.5	—	—
Less-than-4-year degree	83.9	18.2	88.2	1.9
College degree	73.4	25.0	89.9	1.8
Advanced degree	55.8	41.7	76.7	3.3
Amount borrowed for undergraduate education				
None	21.5	90.0	79.4	3.5
Less than $5,000	67.3	32.3	79.3	2.7
$5,000 or more	66.9	28.8	81.6	2.8
Type of institution that granted bachelor's degree				
Private not-for-profit	61.6	37.2	78.8	3.3
Public	70.5	28.4	84.5	2.2
Race–ethnicity				
Native American/Alaska Native	—	—	—	—
Asian/Pacific Islander	56.1	42.2	74.5	3.5
Black	73.2	28.5	85.6	1.9
Hispanic	69.7	33.3	93.1	1.9
White	67.9	30.6	82.0	2.7
Undergraduate major				
Agriculture/home economics	68.0	36.3	—	—
Business	76.8	18.9	79.1	2.0
Journalism/communications	78.4	21.6	83.8	1.9
Education	73.5	35.9	100.0	1.4
Math/computers/engineer	69.4	31.3	92.2	1.8
Health	68.6	19.8	—	—
Sciences (biology, chemistry)	37.6	59.5	78.4	5.2
Sciences (psychology, economics)	54.2	38.9	83.1	3.1
Art/music	77.0	28.9	90.2	1.8
Letters/languages/history	51.1	41.8	75.9	3.3
Other	60.1	40.7	71.5	2.3

—Sample size is too small for a reliable estimate.

SOURCE: National Center for Education Statistics, High School & Beyond: 1980 Sophomore Cohort, 1980–1992.

Section 3

Labor Market Outcomes
of the 1980 Sophomore Class

Labor Force Participation

- Employment rates in February 1992 were higher among 1980 high school sophomores who had earned an associate's, bachelor's, or master's degree or higher than among those with lower levels of educational attainment. Moreover, the employment rates of those with a high school diploma were higher than the rates of those who had not attained a high school. However, there were no significant differences in the percentages of 1980 sophomores who were working among those with associate's, bachelor's, and master's degrees (table 3.1.A).[12]

- Both gender and race–ethnicity appeared to be related to labor force participation. More male respondents than female respondents reported that they were working, and more females than males reported that they were out of the labor force in February 1992. Blacks were less likely than whites to be working, and were more likely than whites to be in the labor force but unemployed and not receiving benefits. However, there were no other significant differences in the rates of employment among the various racial–ethnic groups (table 3.1.A).

- Rates of employment and participation in the labor force among 1980 high school sophomores were not related to their parents' level of educational attainment (table 3.1.A).

- The 1980 high school sophomores who were in the lowest SES and test quartiles were less likely to be working in February 1992 than were those in the middle two or highest quartiles of each measure (table 3.1.A). Among respondents with bachelor's degrees, however, there were no significant differences in employment rates by SES or test scores in high school.[13] Thus, lower rates of employment among sophomores with lower SES or test scores apparently reflected their lower average levels of educational attainment because employment rates in February 1992 were the same for all sophomores with bachelor's degrees, regardless of their SES or test quartile in high school.

---

[12]The percentages of respondents working in the total, marital status, and race–ethnicity categories in table 3.1.A are inconsistent with those shown in table 1.3 because the timing of events reported differs. Table 1.3 reports on the activities of respondents during the week before they were surveyed, while table 3.1.A reports on respondents' activities during the entire month of February 1992.

[13]The total row in table 3.1.B is inconsistent with the bachelor's degree attained row in table 3.1.A because the patterns of missing data for the samples used to generate the two tables are different.

- Males and females in the 1980 sophomore class tended to work in different industries and occupations (table 3.2 and table 3.3). For example, women were more likely to be employed in clerical and service occupations, while men were more likely to be working as technicians.

Annual Earnings

- Earnings were significantly related to the 1980 sophomores' level of educational attainment in 1992. For example, with each successively higher level of educational attainment, the percentage of 1980 sophomores who earned less than $15,000 in 1991 declined (table 3.4).

- Members of the 1980 sophomore class who were married in 1992 had higher average earnings in 1991 than those who were never married or divorced (table 3.5).

- Respondents who had earned bachelor's degrees in the fields of health, math, computers, or engineering had significantly higher average earnings in their first year after degree attainment than did those who studied business, arts, or music (table 3.6.A).

Table 3.1.A—Percentage distribution of 1980 high school sophomores by type of labor force participation in February 1992, by selected characteristics

Student characteristics	Working	Unemployed, receiving benefits	Unemployed, not receiving benefits	Out of labor force
Total	83.1	2.4	4.8	9.7
Highest degree earned by 1992				
Less than high school	69.0	3.8	12.9	14.3
High school	81.9	2.6	5.0	10.5
Certificate	81.3	2.3	5.9	10.5
Associate's	89.7	1.5	2.6	6.1
Bachelor's	89.1	1.8	2.4	6.7
Master's	89.5	1.7	1.1	7.7
Professional	81.1	0.0	1.5	17.4
Doctorate	—	—	—	—
Marital status in 1992				
Married	82.1	1.9	4.0	12.0
Separated	75.2	1.8	10.6	12.4
Divorced	84.6	2.2	4.7	8.5
Widowed	—	—	—	—
Never married	84.8	3.3	5.5	6.4
Living in a marriage-like relationship	89.3	1.1	6.6	3.0
Sex				
Male	90.1	3.0	2.9	4.0
Female	76.3	1.8	6.7	15.2
Socioeconomic status (1980)				
Low quartile	78.6	3.6	6.8	11.0
Middle two quartiles	85.7	1.8	3.6	8.9
High quartile	86.8	1.8	3.0	8.4
Test score composite (1982)				
Low quartile	74.9	3.6	9.1	12.5
Middle two quartiles	85.4	2.4	3.8	8.5
High quartile	88.3	1.2	2.0	8.6
Race–ethnicity				
Native American/Alaska Native	81.6	2.1	4.9	11.5
Asian/Pacific Islander	83.4	1.0	2.0	13.7
Black	77.7	4.2	9.6	8.6
Hispanic	80.5	3.7	5.0	10.9
White	84.5	1.9	4.0	9.6
Parents' educational attainment in 1980				
No high school diploma	83.8	2.5	5.1	8.6
High school graduate	86.5	1.6	4.0	8.0
Vocational/technical	84.7	1.6	4.2	9.5
Some college	85.8	2.1	3.8	8.3
Bachelor's degree	84.9	1.9	3.5	9.7
Advanced degree	83.9	2.9	2.8	10.4

—Sample size is too small for a reliable estimate.

NOTE: Percentages may not sum to 100 percent due to rounding.

SOURCE: National Center for Education Statistics, High School & Beyond: 1980 Sophomore Cohort, 1980–1992.

Table 3.1.B—Percentage distribution of 1980 high school sophomores who had earned bachelor's degrees by 1992, by type of labor force participation in February 1992 and selected characteristics

Student characteristics	Working	Unemployed, receiving benefits	Unemployed, not receiving benefits	Out of labor force
Total	88.9	1.7	2.3	7.2
Marital status in 1992				
Married	88.9	1.0	2.2	7.9
Separated	—	—	—	—
Divorced	94.1	2.9	2.2	0.9
Widowed	—	—	—	—
Never married	88.4	2.5	2.1	6.9
Living in a marriage-like relationship	—	—	—	—
Sex				
Male	91.6	1.8	1.7	4.9
Female	86.3	1.7	2.8	9.3
Socioeconomic status (1980)				
Low quartile	87.5	4.0	3.1	5.4
Middle two quartiles	91.1	1.5	1.9	5.6
High quartile	88.1	1.5	2.4	8.0
Test score composite (1982)				
Low quartile	85.1	0.2	8.8	6.0
Middle two quartiles	89.2	2.7	1.7	6.4
High quartile	88.5	1.3	2.4	7.8
Race–ethnicity				
Native American/Alaska Native	86.7	0.0	3.7	9.6
Asian/Pacific Islander	82.3	0.0	0.6	17.1
Black	86.2	3.2	5.0	5.6
Hispanic	89.4	0.9	1.8	8.0
White	89.2	1.7	2.1	7.0
Parents' educational attainment in 1980				
No high school diploma	91.4	1.9	2.6	4.1
High school graduate	90.6	3.9	0.3	5.3
Vocational/technical	90.9	1.0	2.4	5.7
Some college	89.0	1.6	2.9	6.5
Bachelor's degree	87.7	1.5	1.1	9.8
Advanced degree	84.1	2.2	1.6	12.1

—Sample size is too small for a reliable estimate.

NOTE: Percentages may not sum to 100 percent due to rounding.

SOURCE: National Center for Education Statistics, High School & Beyond: 1980 Sophomore Cohort, 1980–1992.

Table 3.2—Percentage distribution of 1980 high school sophomores, by industry of employment in 1992 and selected characteristics

Student characteristics	Agriculture	Mining	Construction	Manufacture durable goods	Manufacture nondurables	Public utilities	Wholesale trade	Retail trade	Finance	Business services	Personal services	Recreation services	Professional service	Public administration
Total	2.0	0.3	6.4	8.7	4.5	6.0	2.8	13.4	8.2	7.1	13.3	2.2	16.5	8.5
Occupation														
Clerical-secretarial	0.7	0.0	3.3	5.0	3.7	7.8	2.2	6.9	15.1	6.6	10.5	0.8	24.9	12.4
Clerical-financial	2.2	0.6	5.1	3.6	2.3	1.9	3.8	15.2	39.2	6.4	6.1	0.8	7.2	5.6
Clerical-other	0.8	0.5	0.5	5.2	5.2	14.8	3.6	13.7	14.5	8.4	7.0	0.8	14.2	10.9
Craftsman	0.1	0.1	23.2	12.1	7.9	6.8	1.2	7.2	0.3	20.1	11.7	1.0	2.8	5.8
Farmer	85.5	0.0	0.0	5.1	4.2	0.0	0.0	4.1	0.0	0.0	1.2	0.0	0.0	0.0
Homemaker	—	—	—	—	—	—	—	—	—	—	—	—	—	—
Laborer	4.6	0.9	14.3	14.9	7.9	5.8	3.0	11.7	1.0	6.0	21.5	0.9	4.3	3.4
Manager-sales	0.3	0.0	3.2	7.7	4.1	4.9	7.9	37.4	7.6	6.0	12.1	1.8	5.2	1.8
Manager-government	0.0	0.0	2.0	0.7	0.0	14.7	0.0	0.7	11.0	2.8	6.0	0.4	9.9	52.0
Manager-retail	0.0	0.0	0.7	0.9	3.2	0.7	2.9	53.4	1.0	4.2	23.0	7.5	2.3	0.3
Manager-manufacturing	2.4	0.4	32.4	30.6	8.9	3.6	3.2	3.1	2.2	3.4	6.8	0.2	0.2	2.6
Manager-other	2.2	0.3	4.0	8.1	3.8	5.9	2.5	10.0	22.4	10.0	7.2	3.1	13.6	6.8
Military	0.0	0.0	0.5	0.3	0.0	5.5	0.0	0.9	0.0	0.6	0.3	0.0	13.9	78.0
Skilled operative	2.3	0.8	7.8	23.4	8.7	14.8	5.6	6.1	1.3	9.4	10.4	0.8	4.5	4.3
Professional-arts	1.7	0.0	0.3	4.4	1.7	10.2	1.1	4.4	2.8	13.2	15.5	29.2	11.8	3.8
Professional-medical	0.4	0.0	0.0	0.4	0.1	0.1	0.8	1.3	0.4	0.8	9.2	0.2	81.7	4.8
Professional-engineer	0.8	0.0	12.6	43.5	8.3	6.0	0.8	1.4	1.3	3.3	5.2	0.3	6.3	10.2
Physician	0.0	0.0	0.0	0.0	0.0	0.0	0.0	1.7	0.0	1.3	5.3	0.0	78.1	13.7
Professional-legal	0.0	0.0	1.1	0.0	0.1	0.0	0.0	0.8	4.6	14.5	15.0	0.0	45.5	18.5
Professional-other	2.4	0.0	0.1	3.6	2.9	4.3	0.7	3.4	18.3	5.2	7.6	3.5	39.0	9.2
Owner-retail	0.0	0.0	0.0	0.0	0.8	0.2	0.0	66.1	0.0	6.7	24.1	2.0	0.1	0.0
Owner-manufacturing	4.3	0.0	62.4	9.6	4.4	0.0	1.0	8.8	0.0	3.4	6.1	0.0	0.0	0.0
Owner-other	9.6	0.1	3.6	6.3	1.3	5.2	3.1	10.5	6.8	7.6	32.7	4.5	7.4	1.4
Protective services	1.0	0.0	0.8	0.8	0.0	2.1	0.0	2.3	0.7	2.7	8.5	1.9	14.1	65.2
Sales	0.7	0.0	0.5	5.7	6.9	4.0	9.1	40.4	12.7	8.1	7.2	2.1	2.5	0.3
School teacher	0.0	0.0	0.0	0.0	0.0	0.0	0.0	0.2	0.7	0.7	5.5	0.4	76.5	15.9
Service	0.0	0.0	0.2	0.6	1.6	4.2	0.7	18.8	1.3	2.6	37.3	5.4	24.8	2.5
Tech-computer related	0.0	0.0	0.2	16.0	3.9	11.4	3.7	6.8	19.1	11.6	4.6	0.6	12.3	10.0
Tech-noncomputer related	0.3	1.3	2.5	6.8	2.7	13.4	0.5	5.7	4.5	12.9	8.8	2.5	29.9	8.4
Highest degree earned by 1992														
Less than high school	4.0	0.0	10.9	10.7	13.0	3.5	3.0	16.7	2.3	8.0	19.1	1.2	3.9	3.8
High school	2.3	0.4	8.4	9.7	4.3	6.3	3.4	15.9	6.0	7.2	14.0	2.4	11.3	8.3
Certificate	1.1	0.2	6.6	5.6	3.1	6.4	1.7	12.1	7.6	8.9	18.4	1.7	17.7	8.9
Associate's	2.0	0.2	4.5	8.5	5.0	7.8	2.7	11.4	7.0	7.1	13.9	2.7	21.6	5.7
Bachelor's	1.5	0.1	2.6	7.5	3.8	5.8	2.5	9.9	15.1	6.4	8.2	2.4	23.4	10.7
Master's	1.0	0.0	0.9	10.5	5.4	4.5	0.8	4.7	10.9	2.8	8.6	1.6	39.5	8.8
Professional	0.0	0.0	0.0	2.1	0.5	0.5	0.0	1.9	1.1	12.3	14.2	0.0	47.2	20.3
Doctorate	—	—	—	—	—	—	—	—	—	—	—	—	—	—

Table 3.2—Percentage distribution of 1980 high school sophomores, by industry of employment in 1992 and selected characteristics—Continued

Student characteristics	Agriculture	Mining	Construction	Manufacture durable goods	Manufacture nondurables	Public utilities	Wholesale trade	Retail trade	Finance	Business services	Personal services	Recreation services	Professional service	Public administration
Marital status in 1992														
Married	2.0	0.2	6.3	9.3	4.9	6.0	3.1	12.1	8.5	7.0	12.5	1.6	17.1	9.6
Separated	1.4	0.0	8.4	8.6	3.9	4.4	1.5	17.2	6.5	6.7	14.9	3.3	15.5	7.9
Divorced	1.4	1.0	10.3	11.5	4.2	7.1	2.4	12.2	4.6	6.2	14.0	2.9	13.9	8.6
Widowed	—	—	—	—	—	—	—	—	—	—	—	—	—	—
Never married	2.2	0.3	5.7	7.4	4.3	5.8	2.5	15.4	8.5	7.4	14.0	2.9	16.3	7.3
Living in a marriage-like relationship	3.4	0.0	8.0	6.8	1.0	9.2	6.2	9.6	4.6	11.6	13.5	5.9	12.2	8.1
Sex														
Male	3.2	0.4	10.6	11.1	4.6	7.5	3.4	12.8	5.1	8.9	11.8	2.3	8.7	9.7
Female	0.6	0.2	1.5	5.9	4.5	4.3	2.2	14.0	11.7	5.0	15.2	2.1	25.5	7.2
Race–ethnicity														
Native American/Alaska Native	2.9	0.0	7.4	8.9	2.8	4.4	1.1	15.1	4.4	3.4	22.4	3.0	15.8	8.5
Asian/Pacific Islander	0.8	0.0	1.1	7.7	3.8	8.5	1.4	15.3	9.0	5.3	15.3	4.0	20.2	7.8
Black	1.3	0.0	3.3	6.7	4.2	9.4	2.4	10.3	7.0	5.5	15.9	2.1	17.7	14.1
Hispanic	2.0	0.7	6.1	8.5	6.3	5.7	2.7	15.7	6.8	5.7	14.2	1.3	15.7	8.7
White	2.1	0.3	6.8	9.0	4.5	5.6	3.0	13.6	8.5	7.4	12.6	2.3	16.5	7.7

—Sample size is too small for a reliable estimate.

NOTE: Percentages may not sum to 100 percent due to rounding.

SOURCE: National Center for Education Statistics, High School & Beyond: 1980 Sophomore Cohort, 1980–1992.

Table 3.3—Percentage distribution of 1980 high school sophomores, by occupation in 1992 and selected characteristics

Student characteristic	Clerical	Craftsman	Farmer	Home-maker	Laborer	Manager	Military	Skilled operative	Profes-sional	Owner	Protective services	Sales	School teacher	Service	Tech-nical
Total	15.8	6.4	0.4	0.1	15.1	17.0	1.8	5.9	12.5	2.6	2.1	6.6	2.3	6.9	4.7
Industry															
Agriculture	9.2	0.3	17.6	0.0	34.9	11.4	0.0	6.8	7.1	8.9	1.0	2.5	0.0	0.0	0.2
Mining	—	—	—	—	—	—	—	—	—	—	—	—	—	—	—
Construction	7.4	23.2	0.0	0.0	33.9	17.9	0.2	7.2	3.0	5.6	0.3	0.5	0.0	0.2	0.7
Manufacture durable goods	8.5	8.9	0.2	0.0	25.8	17.6	0.1	15.8	9.5	1.7	0.2	4.3	0.0	0.5	6.9
Manufacture nondurables	13.0	11.1	0.4	0.0	26.1	15.7	0.0	11.3	5.5	1.0	0.0	9.9	0.0	2.5	3.6
Public utilities	21.4	7.2	0.0	0.0	14.4	13.6	1.7	14.5	6.8	1.4	0.7	4.3	0.0	4.8	9.3
Wholesale trade	16.8	2.6	0.0	0.0	15.8	21.1	0.0	11.6	3.2	1.9	0.0	21.0	0.0	1.8	4.3
Retail trade	13.0	3.4	0.1	0.0	13.2	28.8	0.1	2.7	2.2	4.4	0.4	19.8	0.0	9.7	2.2
Finance	41.3	0.2	0.0	0.0	1.9	25.1	0.0	0.9	9.5	1.3	0.2	10.2	0.2	1.1	8.0
Business services	15.5	18.0	0.0	0.1	12.6	16.3	0.1	7.7	8.3	2.5	0.8	7.4	0.2	2.6	7.9
Personal services	9.8	5.6	0.0	0.2	24.3	14.3	0.0	4.6	8.7	5.2	1.3	3.5	1.0	19.3	2.1
Recreation services	5.7	2.9	0.0	0.0	5.9	24.7	0.0	2.0	27.3	3.8	1.8	6.3	0.5	16.6	2.6
Professional service	16.3	1.1	0.0	0.0	4.0	8.1	1.5	1.6	37.7	0.7	1.8	1.0	10.7	10.4	5.2
Public administration	18.6	4.3	0.0	0.2	6.0	12.6	16.4	3.0	11.1	0.3	16.0	0.2	4.3	2.0	5.1
Highest degree earned by 1992															
Less than high school	4.3	13.9	0.4	0.0	39.7	9.9	0.0	9.8	2.9	2.4	0.1	6.8	0.6	8.9	0.5
High school	17.4	7.7	0.5	0.1	20.7	15.8	2.3	7.9	4.6	3.2	2.5	6.3	0.6	7.4	2.9
Certificate	19.6	10.5	0.1	0.0	13.7	9.3	1.4	6.1	10.1	3.0	3.2	4.9	0.4	13.6	4.2
Associate's	21.5	5.8	1.0	0.3	8.9	18.5	0.8	4.1	15.4	2.0	1.8	5.0	0.3	7.5	7.3
Bachelor's	13.0	1.2	0.2	0.0	2.9	24.7	1.9	1.7	25.5	1.9	1.4	8.8	7.1	2.2	7.8
Master's	4.3	0.0	0.0	0.0	0.7	20.0	0.0	0.9	40.8	1.6	1.0	3.8	11.3	3.1	12.4
Professional	3.0	0.0	0.0	0.0	0.0	3.3	2.5	1.8	78.7	3.5	2.6	2.5	0.5	0.5	1.1
Doctorate	—	—	—	—	—	—	—	—	—	—	—	—	—	—	—
Marital status in 1992															
Married	17.0	6.7	0.4	0.0	13.3	17.6	2.1	5.8	12.0	2.9	1.9	6.4	2.3	6.5	5.1
Separated	18.3	9.1	0.0	0.0	21.9	7.3	3.0	9.0	8.5	3.0	0.6	7.6	0.8	10.0	1.0
Divorced	15.1	6.6	0.0	0.0	20.0	13.9	3.1	6.5	11.0	3.1	2.2	5.5	1.3	8.8	2.8
Widowed	—	—	—	—	—	—	—	—	—	—	—	—	—	—	—
Never married	13.6	5.8	0.5	0.1	16.2	16.7	1.1	6.0	14.0	2.3	2.5	7.3	2.5	7.0	4.6
Living in a marriage-like relationship	15.2	7.7	0.0	0.0	31.1	17.9	0.6	4.3	5.6	0.0	1.9	2.1	1.8	11.0	0.7
Sex															
Male	4.8	10.6	0.7	0.1	21.4	17.7	3.0	8.7	9.7	3.3	3.2	6.4	1.0	4.0	5.6
Female	28.5	1.4	0.1	0.0	7.9	16.0	0.4	2.8	15.7	1.9	0.8	6.8	3.9	10.3	3.5

Table 3.3—Percentage distribution of 1980 high school sophomores, by occupation in 1992 and selected characteristics—Continued

Student characteristic	Clerical	Craftsman	Farmer	Home-maker	Laborer	Manager	Military	Skilled operative	Profes-sional	Owner	Protective services	Sales	School teacher	Service	Tech-nical
Race-ethnicity															
Native American/ Alaska Native	10.0	14.6	0.0	0.6	26.5	13.7	0.9	5.6	7.5	2.3	4.0	5.5	2.0	4.3	2.6
Asian/Pacific Islander	19.5	2.3	0.0	0.0	8.9	14.0	1.6	6.2	21.3	4.0	2.6	2.4	0.9	10.6	5.8
Black	18.6	4.7	0.1	0.0	20.8	11.0	3.1	6.6	10.5	0.9	4.1	3.8	1.7	10.9	3.3
Hispanic	17.9	6.4	0.5	0.0	21.9	14.0	1.6	6.2	8.0	1.9	3.1	6.8	1.5	6.8	3.5
White	15.2	6.5	0.5	0.1	13.3	18.1	1.7	5.8	13.2	3.0	1.7	7.2	2.5	6.3	5.0

—Sample size is too small for a reliable estimate.

NOTE: Percentages may not sum to 100 percent due to rounding.

SOURCE: National Center for Education Statistics, High School & Beyond: 1980 Sophomore Cohort, 1980–1992.

Table 3.4—Percentage distribution of 1980 high school sophomores, by annual earnings in 1991 and selected characteristics

Student characteristics	Less than $15,000	$15,000–$29,999	$30,000–$49,999	$50,000–$74,999	$75,000 or more
Total	29.1	48.4	19.7	2.2	0.7
Highest degree earned by 1992					
Less than high school	51.1	38.8	8.6	1.4	0.1
High school	33.1	49.7	14.9	1.5	0.7
Certificate	32.7	49.8	16.1	0.6	0.8
Associate's	24.3	55.8	18.4	1.1	0.4
Bachelor's	16.3	46.5	33.3	3.4	0.5
Master's	19.4	33.1	36.3	9.1	2.1
Professional	16.2	31.3	34.7	13.4	4.4
Doctorate	—	—	—	—	—
Marital status in 1992					
Married	27.7	49.4	20.3	2.1	0.6
Separated	44.8	43.2	11.9	0.1	0.1
Divorced	35.2	49.8	13.7	0.5	0.9
Widowed	—	—	—	—	—
Never married	29.0	47.6	20.0	2.7	0.8
Living in a marriage-like relationship	32.0	51.9	14.3	1.9	0.0
Sex					
Male	21.9	49.0	25.1	3.1	1.0
Female	37.3	47.6	13.6	1.1	0.4
Amount still owed for education					
None	29.5	48.9	18.8	2.0	0.8
Less than $1,000	26.9	46.8	24.8	1.5	0.0
$1,000 or more	26.9	45.7	23.8	3.4	0.3
Occupation in 1992					
Clerical	31.6	57.3	9.8	0.7	0.6
Craftsman	19.0	57.1	21.3	1.7	1.0
Farmer	—	—	—	—	—
Homemaker	—	—	—	—	—
Laborer	39.6	46.1	12.9	1.2	0.1
Manager	12.9	53.3	29.5	3.6	0.7
Military	17.7	59.3	22.1	0.9	0.0
Skilled operative	18.4	59.9	19.7	1.9	0.0
Professional	20.1	44.4	30.8	3.9	0.9
Owner	27.4	37.8	19.6	10.5	4.7
Protective services	23.5	46.0	28.9	1.7	0.0
Sales	32.8	41.9	21.0	3.8	0.5
School teacher	34.9	57.7	7.4	0.0	0.0
Service	53.6	38.3	7.3	0.3	0.6
Technical	8.8	42.0	46.1	2.3	0.9
Race–ethnicity					
Native American/Alaska Native	46.9	39.5	10.9	0.7	2.0
Asian/Pacific Islander	18.6	47.3	28.4	3.9	1.7
Black	37.0	46.7	14.0	1.9	0.5
Hispanic	32.0	49.4	16.2	1.7	0.7
White	27.7	48.3	21.0	2.3	0.7

—Sample size is too small for a reliable estimate.

NOTE: Percentages may not sum to 100 percent due to rounding.

SOURCE: National Center for Education Statistics, High School & Beyond: 1980 Sophomore Cohort, 1980–1992.

Table 3.5—Average earnings among 1980 high school sophomores in their first year after terminating their education, by highest degree attained and selected characteristics

Student characteristics	High school	Certificate	Associate's	Bachelor's	Advanced degree	Average earnings, all degrees
Total	$15,729	$15,014	$17,785	$21,356	$26,122	$18,028
Marital status in 1992						
Married	16,962	16,227	18,889	22,385	27,310	19,042
Separated	12,714	13,370	—	—	—	14,858
Divorced	14,160	14,505	18,582	20,147	—	15,853
Widowed	—	—	—	—	—	—
Never married	13,708	13,162	15,731	20,371	24,861	16,859
Living in a marriage-like relationship	—	—	—	—	—	16,696
Sex						
Male	17,286	18,155	17,870	23,341	28,181	19,918
Female	14,293	12,659	17,725	19,500	23,759	16,367
Repeated grade/held back in school						
Never repeated	13,836	15,304	17,930	20,771	—	16,334
Repeated grade	16,191	15,386	17,877	21,627	25,952	18,526
Race-ethnicity						
Native American/Alaska Native	17,714	9,428	—	—	—	15,426
Asian/Pacific Islander	16,177	—	—	21,096	27,762	19,607
Black	13,724	13,170	14,181	19,721	22,127	14,775
Hispanic	14,284	14,752	17,536	21,811	25,893	16,216
White	16,283	15,737	18,391	21,478	26,564	18,736

—Sample size is too small for a reliable estimate.

SOURCE: National Center for Education Statistics, High School & Beyond: 1980 Sophomore Cohort, 1980–1992.

Table 3.6.A—Average earnings among 1980 high school sophomores in their first and third year after attaining a bachelor's degree, by selected characteristics

Student characteristics	Earnings in first year after bachelor's degree	Earnings in third year after bachelor's degree
Total	$20,932	$24,215
Sex		
Male	22,649	27,190
Female	19,362	21,526
Institution control where earned bachelor's degree		
Private not-for-profit	21,682	25,199
Public	20,931	24,082
Race–ethnicity		
Native American/Alaska Native	—	—
Asian/Pacific Islander	20,798	25,442
Black	20,112	21,199
Hispanic	22,436	25,463
White	20,984	24,372
Undergraduate major		
Agriculture/home economics	21,802	21,588
Business	21,634	25,494
Journalism/communications	19,222	22,687
Education	16,295	18,526
Math/computers/engineering	26,643	30,442
Health	27,253	29,467
Sciences (biology, chemistry)	19,339	21,559
Sciences (psychology, economics)	18,875	21,902
Art/music	16,945	19,210
Letters/languages/history	17,357	21,560
Other	18,328	20,754

—Sample size is too small for a reliable estimate.

NOTE: All estimates are in 1992 dollars.

SOURCE: National Center for Education Statistics, High School & Beyond: 1980 Sophomore Cohort, 1980–1992.

Table 3.6.B—Average earnings among 1980 high school graduates in their first and third year after attaining an associate's degree, by selected characteristics

Student characteristics	Earnings in first year after associate's degree	Earnings in third year after associate's degree
Total	$16,912	$20,093
Sex		
Male	17,054	21,685
Female	16,813	18,988
Race–ethnicity		
Native American/Alaska Native	—	—
Asian/Pacific Islander	—	—
Black	13,655	15,550
Hispanic	15,590	25,163
White	17,614	20,302
Undergraduate major		
Agriculture/home economics	—	—
Business	16,813	17,940
Journalism/communications	—	—
Education	—	—
Math/computers/engineer	16,785	19,220
Health	20,911	23,346
Sciences (biology, chemistry)	—	—
Sciences (psychology, economics)	—	—
Art/music	—	—
Letters/languages/history	—	—
Other	14,805	17,225

—Sample size is too small for a reliable estimate.

NOTE: All estimates are in 1992 dollars.

SOURCE: National Center for Education Statistics, High School & Beyond: 1980 Sophomore Cohort, 1980–1992.

Table 3.6.C—Average earnings among 1980 high school sophomores in their first and third year after attaining a postsecondary certificate, by selected characteristics

Student characteristics	Earnings in first year after certificate	Earnings in third year after certificate
Total	$14,526	$17,551
Sex		
Male	17,437	21,137
Female	12,266	14,869
Race–ethnicity		
Native American/Alaska Native	10,529	—
Asian/Pacific Islander	—	—
Black	12,869	14,611
Hispanic	14,593	14,532
White	15,145	18,712
Undergraduate major		
Agriculture/home economics	—	—
Business	12,956	15,444
Journalism/communications	—	—
Education	—	—
Math/computers/engineering	16,284	18,947
Health	15,364	18,101
Sciences (biology, chemistry)	—	—
Sciences (psychology, economics)	—	—
Art/music	—	—
Letters/languages/history	—	—
Other	13,879	19,514

—Sample size is too small for a reliable estimate.

NOTE: All estimates are in 1992 dollars.

SOURCE: National Center for Education Statistics, High School & Beyond: 1980 Sophomore Cohort, 1980–1992.

Section 4

Voting Behavior, Attitudes, and Family Formation
of the 1980 Sophomore Class

Voting Behavior

- Roughly 65 percent of 1980 high school sophomores were registered to vote in 1986 and 1992. Fifty-three percent of all sophomores voted in the 1988 presidential election, while only one-third voted in any other 1988 elections. More respondents voted in the 1988 presidential election than in the 1984 election (table 4.1).

- The 1980 high school sophomores' voting rates in the 1988 elections were positively associated with educational attainment: as attainment increased, the percentage who voted also increased. For example, 25 percent of those with less than a high school education voted in the 1988 presidential election, compared with 46 percent of those with a high school diploma (table 4.1).

Attitudes

- Questions about the values held by the 1980 sophomores reveal that more than 95 percent of all 1980 high school sophomores felt that success in work, having steady work, strong friendships, and better opportunities for their children were important. By contrast, only about half (56 percent) said that having money was important (table 4.2).

- Males were significantly more likely than females to feel that success in work, steady work, and money were important, and were equally as likely as women to value friendship and children's opportunities (table 4.2).

Family Formation

- Respondents who rated themselves as "very popular" in 1982 (when most of them were high school seniors) were more likely to never have been married than those who rated themselves "somewhat popular" (table 4.3).

- Approximately half the 1980 high school sophomores had at least one child by 1992, while nearly 10 percent had at least three children. The rate of parenting varied by gender, however, and males were significantly more likely than females to report having no children (table 4.4).

Table 4.1—Voting indicators for 1980 high school sophomores, by selected characteristics

Student characteristics	Percent registered in 1986	Percent registered in 1992	Percent voted 1984 presidential	Percent voted 1988 in non-presidential	Percent voted 1988 presidential
Total	66.9	65.0	48.8	33.5	52.7
Political beliefs in 1980					
Conservative	75.6	75.5	58.3	42.2	65.7
Moderate	69.9	70.0	56.0	40.3	60.8
Liberal	74.4	71.2	60.3	37.7	62.1
Radical	72.4	67.2	50.3	36.0	52.3
None	57.7	57.6	39.3	27.6	44.4
Highest degree earned by 1992					
Less than high school	46.1	43.0	24.1	14.4	25.3
High school	61.6	61.1	43.0	29.9	46.2
Certificate	67.6	65.1	48.0	35.1	53.0
Associate's	69.3	71.2	56.9	39.4	60.4
Bachelor's	80.2	76.0	63.8	43.4	72.0
Master's	87.3	85.3	65.9	49.7	75.6
Professional	79.4	81.2	63.7	42.0	70.6
Doctorate	—	—	—	—	—
Marital status in 1992					
Married	65.5	64.3	47.4	33.2	52.7
Separated	65.2	54.1	41.5	22.7	38.7
Divorced	57.0	55.5	36.9	22.9	40.0
Widowed	—	—	—	—	—
Never married	70.6	68.2	53.4	36.3	56.1
Living in a marriage-like relationship	63.4	62.9	45.5	35.6	47.4
Sex					
Male	67.2	64.2	48.2	32.2	51.5
Female	66.5	65.8	49.4	34.9	53.9
Race–ethnicity					
Native American/ Alaska Native	64.5	65.6	41.4	29.4	40.2
Asian/Pacific Islander	50.6	56.8	33.2	25.7	39.9
Black	73.9	70.7	51.2	36.1	51.3
Hispanic	62.4	63.0	41.3	29.8	43.3
White	66.6	64.5	49.7	33.7	54.6

—Sample size is too small for a reliable estimate.

SOURCE: National Center for Education Statistics, High School & Beyond: 1980 Sophomore Cohort, 1980–1992.

Table 4.2—Percentage of 1980 high school sophomores who reported in 1992 that they valued the specified items in their lives, by selected characteristics

Student characteristics	Success in their work	Steady work	Money	Strong friendships	Making their children better off
Total	95.9	95.6	55.6	95.2	96.5
Marital and parental status in 1992					
Married no children	96.8	97.7	55.2	97.5	95.8
Married with children	95.6	93.5	52.3	95.0	98.6
Divorced/sep/widow no children	97.2	98.7	50.8	95.3	93.0
Divorced/sep/widow with children	95.6	95.5	56.2	91.5	98.4
Never married no children	95.9	96.5	57.9	96.6	93.9
Never married with children	95.6	96.6	62.3	88.3	98.0
Living together no children	99.8	98.1	46.8	100.0	95.4
Living together with children	95.7	99.7	76.6	94.3	100.0
Highest degree earned by 1992					
Less than high school	95.4	95.3	63.8	94.2	99.6
High school	95.3	95.2	56.2	94.4	97.5
Certificate	96.8	95.2	57.1	94.0	98.0
Associate's	96.3	97.5	56.5	96.2	97.5
Bachelor's	96.6	96.0	49.7	98.2	93.0
Master's	98.4	96.3	49.8	98.1	89.4
Professional	98.4	99.5	50.7	99.7	96.8
Doctorate	—	—	—	—	—
Sex					
Male	97.3	97.4	60.1	95.1	96.2
Female	94.5	93.9	51.2	95.3	96.8
Race–ethnicity					
Native American/ Alaska Native	97.4	93.5	57.7	96.3	96.8
Asian/Pacific Islander	95.9	97.6	58.3	98.2	97.1
Black	96.3	96.5	66.0	85.1	98.1
Hispanic	97.1	95.6	61.5	92.2	98.4
White	95.7	95.4	52.9	97.2	96.0

—Sample size is too small for a reliable estimate.

SOURCE: National Center for Education Statistics, High School & Beyond: 1980 Sophomore Cohort, 1980–1992.

Table 4.3—Percentage distribution of 1980 high school sophomores, by number of times they had been married by 1992 and selected characteristics

Student characteristics	Never married	One	Two	Three or more
Total	37.9	56.8	5.1	0.3
Sex				
Male	45.5	50.8	3.7	0.1
Female	30.7	62.4	6.3	0.6
Race–ethnicity				
Native American/Alaska Native	36.5	51.5	11.7	0.3
Asian/Pacific Islander	49.4	46.8	3.8	0.0
Black	55.2	41.7	3.1	0.1
White	34.7	59.5	5.4	0.4
Hispanic-Mexican	40.4	56.3	3.2	0.0
Hispanic-Cuban	37.7	58.2	4.2	0.0
Hispanic-Puerto Rican	44.6	51.2	3.7	0.5
Hispanic-other	36.0	59.2	4.8	0.0
Religious background in 1980				
Baptist	32.4	59.3	8.1	0.3
Methodist	34.2	60.4	5.2	0.2
Lutheran	34.3	61.8	3.9	0.1
Presbyterian	34.0	61.9	3.7	0.4
Episcopalian	48.5	45.8	5.7	0.0
Other Protestant	31.1	65.2	3.6	0.1
Catholic	41.8	54.5	3.6	0.1
Other Christian	32.0	59.9	6.6	1.5
Jewish	62.0	33.9	3.6	0.6
Other religion	29.9	64.4	4.4	1.4
None	44.4	50.6	4.5	0.5
Popularity in 1982				
Very popular	44.2	52.7	3.1	0.0
Somewhat popular	37.0	57.6	5.0	0.3
Not at all popular	38.9	56.4	4.7	0.1

NOTE: Percentages may not sum to 100 percent due to rounding.

SOURCE: National Center for Education Statistics, High School & Beyond: 1980 Sophomore Cohort, 1980–1992.

Table 4.4—Percentage distribution of 1980 sophomores, by the number of children parented through 1992 and selected characteristics

	None	One	Two	Three or four	Five or more
Total	48.9	21.3	20.1	9.4	0.2
Marital status in 1992					
Married	29.7	27.8	28.8	13.4	0.3
Separated	20.6	24.8	32.7	21.2	0.7
Divorced	32.4	30.0	26.9	10.5	0.3
Widowed	—	—	—	—	—
Never married	81.0	10.0	6.0	3.0	0.1
Living in a marriage-like relationship	46.3	23.7	17.0	12.9	0.1
Sex					
Male	56.2	19.1	16.8	7.7	0.1
Female	41.8	23.5	23.3	11.1	0.4
Race–ethnicity					
Native American/Alaska Native	33.5	16.4	31.9	17.8	0.4
Asian/Pacific Islander	62.4	23.1	8.5	6.0	0.0
Black	36.7	25.8	21.9	15.2	0.4
White	51.9	20.3	19.6	8.0	0.2
Hispanic-Mexican	41.7	23.4	19.9	15.0	0.0
Hispanic-Cuban	51.4	20.8	19.9	7.9	0.0
Hispanic-Puerto Rican	44.5	21.8	23.9	9.6	0.2
Hispanic-other	41.7	24.4	21.9	12.1	0.0
Religious background in 1980					
Baptist	40.4	22.8	25.1	11.5	0.2
Methodist	47.8	25.3	20.8	5.8	0.3
Lutheran	54.4	19.0	17.8	8.6	0.3
Presbyterian	56.2	19.7	20.0	4.1	0.0
Episcopalian	68.1	14.9	13.9	3.2	0.0
Other Protestant	54.9	20.1	15.8	8.7	0.6
Catholic	57.2	20.2	15.3	7.3	0.1
Other Christian	40.1	22.4	23.8	13.6	0.1
Jewish	80.0	10.4	6.0	3.7	0.0
Other religion	38.9	19.4	25.2	16.0	0.5
None	46.7	23.0	18.5	11.5	0.3
Number of marriages					
Never married	81.1	9.9	6.0	2.9	0.1
One	31.4	28.5	28.1	11.7	0.2
Two	16.5	24.5	30.3	27.1	1.7
Three or more	14.6	33.8	25.2	14.6	11.9

—Sample size is too small for a reliable estimate.

SOURCE: National Center for Education Statistics, High School & Beyond: 1980 Sophomore Cohort, 1980–1992.

Appendix A: Glossary

Appendix A
Glossary

This glossary describes the variables used in this report. These items were taken directly from the HS&B Fourth Followup Data Analysis System (DAS), an NCES software application that generates tables directly from Fourth Followup data files. A description of the DAS files can be found in appendix B.

The variables and definitions are divided into the following categories: postsecondary education variables, other education variables, demographic and status variables, employment variables, and other variables. The variables are organized within each category in alphabetic order by item name.

Postsecondary Education Variables

Accepted at 1982 first choice college (SY14B1)

No applications	Student did not apply to college in 1982.
Attended first choice college	Student was accepted and attended first choice school in 1982.
Accepted but did not attend	Student was accepted at first choice school in 1982, but did not attend at that time.
Was not accepted at first choice	Student was denied admission to first choice school.

Accepted at first choice graduate school (Y4210)

Yes

No

Don't know yet

Amount still owed for education (Y4216)

The amount still owed for education is stored as a continuous variable in the HS&B Fourth Followup Data Analysis System file.

Applied to graduate or professional institution (Y4206)

Yes

No

Entry status (Y4203C01)

Immediate entrants	Students who first entered postsecondary education before November 1982.
Delayed entrants	Students who first entered postsecondary education after October 1982.

First postsecondary institution type (composite of ATNDTYPA–ATNDTYPE)

Never enrolled	Student never enrolled in postsecondary education
Private for-profit	Student first attended a private for-profit (proprietary) institution. A private for-profit institution is a postsecondary institution that is privately owned and operated as a profit-making enterprise. Includes career colleges and proprietary institutions.
Private NFP less-than-4-year	Student first attended a private not-for-profit institution offering a less-than-4-year degree. A private, not-for-profit institution is a postsecondary institution that is controlled by an independent governing board and incorporated under section 501(c)(3) of the Internal Revenue Code.
Public less-than-2-year	Student first attended a public less-than-2-year (vocational-technical) institution. A public institution is a postsecondary education institution operated by publicly elected or appointed officials in which the program and activities are under the control of these officials and which is supported primarily by public funds.
Public 2-year	Student first attended a public institution offering a 2- to 3-year degree (i.e., associate's degree).
Public 4-year	Student first attended a public college or university offering a bachelor's degree or higher.
Private not-for-profit 4-year	Student first attended a private not-for-profit college or university offering a bachelor's degree or higher.

First postsecondary institution start date (derived from MONSTRT)

The MONSTRT variable records the number of months between June 1982 and the student's first entry into postsecondary education. This variable was used to derive the categories in the first institution start date variable.

Never enrolled

Before November 1982

November 1982 to May 1983

June 1983 to May 1984

June 1984 to May 1986

June 1986 or later

Intensity of initial enrollment (Y4203G01)

Full-time   Students who reported that they enrolled full time in the first institution that they attended.

Part-time   Students who reported that they enrolled less than full time in the first institution that they attended.

Highest degree attained by 1992 (HGHDG92)

This variable is a composite that summarizes the highest degree attained by 1980 high school sophomores as of June 1992. The variable categories are mutually exclusive, so each student is included in only one category. Students who did not earn a postsecondary certificate or degree may have attended a postsecondary institution at some time between 1982 and 1992, and students who earned a degree might have enrolled in an institution offering a higher degree than the one that they earned without completing the program by June 1992. Likewise, students in higher degree attainment categories may have also earned a lower degree as well, even though it is not reflected in this variable. In several tables, the master's degree, professional degree, and doctorate categories were combined into a single advanced degree category.

Less than high school graduate   Student did not complete high school.

High school graduate only   Student completed high school.

Vocational certificate   Student completed a vocational certificate, diploma, or award.

Associate's degree	Student completed an associate's degree.
Bachelor's degree	Student completed a bachelor's degree.
Master's degree	Student completed a master's degree.
Professional degree	Student completed a professional degree.
Doctorate	Student completed a doctorate.

Number of applications to college in 1982 (FY124)

Did not apply	Student did not apply to any colleges in 1982.
One college	Student applied to one college in 1982.
2–3 colleges	Student applied to two or three colleges in 1982.
4 or more colleges	Student applied to four or more colleges in 1982.

Number of applications to graduate school (Y4208)

This is a continuous variable that records the number of applications for graduate school that 1980 sophomores reported.

Number of postsecondary institutions attended prior to highest degree attainment in 1992 (composite of PSSCHLA–PSSCHLF)

The number of schools attended prior to degree attainment is specified both in relation to the type of degree attained and across all degree types. The average number of institutions attended by degree type or across all types of degrees include only those students who had attained a degree; students who attended but did not attain a degree were not included in the calculation. The number of schools was determined by asking students how many schools they had attended and by matching institutional identification numbers (FICE codes) to ensure that multiple spells of attendance at one school were not counted as more than one school.

Number of spells of enrollment prior to highest degree attainment in 1992 (ENROLSPL)

ENROLSPL is a composite variable that summarizes across degree types the number of spells of enrollment experienced by students prior to their highest degree attainment; the number of spells is determined for each type of degree by PSSPELLA–PSSPELLF. A single spell of enrollment was defined as any number of months of enrollment that did not include breaks of longer than one month (i.e., attendance was not recorded for any part of two adjacent months), excluding summer (i.e., the student was enrolled in the last standard term of an academic year and the first standard term of the following academic year). A single spell could include attendance at more than one school, provided the break between enrollments did not exceed one month or was not longer than the break between academic years.

Postsecondary expectations in 1982 (PSEPLANS)

This variable describes the highest degree students planned to get at the time they were surveyed in 1982, when most of the 1980 sophomores were high school seniors.

None	Student did not expect to pursue postsecondary education.
Vocational/technical	Student planned to earn a vocational/technical certificate, diploma, or award.
Less-than 4-year degree	Student planned to earn a less-than-4-year degree, most commonly an associate's degree.
College degree	Student planned to earn a bachelor's degree.
Advanced degree	Student planned to earn a master's degree, professional degree, or doctorate.

Took graduate or professional exams (Y4207A)

The 1980 sophomores were asked in the 1992 survey whether they had taken a graduate or professional admission examination. Types of examinations included Dental Admission Test, Graduate Management Admission Test, Graduate Record Examination, Law School Admission Test, Medical College Admission Test, or other admission test.

Type of postsecondary institution (Y4203A01)

4-year institutions	Includes 4-year private, not-for-profit and 4-year public institutions that offer bachelor's degrees or higher. These institutions may also offer associate's degrees or vocational certificates.
Public 2-year institutions	Includes public 2- to 3-year institutions that offer associate's degrees or vocational certificates.
Other institutions	Includes private, for-profit (proprietary) institutions, public less-than-2-year institutions, and private, not-for-profit less-than-4-year institutions.

Type of start in postsecondary education (PSESTART)

This is a composite variable that combines type of institution, intensity of initial enrollment, and timing of initial enrollment into a single variable.

No enrollment
: Student did not enroll in postsecondary education.

Full-time 4-year, fall 1982
: Student enrolled full time in a private, not-for-profit or public 4-year institution before November 1982.

Full-time public 2-year, fall 1982
: Student enrolled full time in a public 2- to 3-year institution before November 1982.

Part-time 4-year, fall 1982
: Student enrolled part time in a private, not-for-profit or public 4-year institution before November 1982.

Part-time public 2-year, fall 1982
: Student enrolled part time in a public 2- to 3-year institution before November 1982.

Delay 4-year
: Student enrolled full time or part time in a private, not-for-profit or public 4-year institution after October 1982.

Delay public 2-year
: Student enrolled full time or part time in a public 2- to 3-year institution after October 1982.

Less-than-2-year, fall 1982
: Student enrolled full time or part time before November 1982 in a private, not-for-profit less-than-2-year institution; a private, for-profit less-than-2-year institution; or a public less-than-2-year institution.

Delay, less-than-2-year
: Student enrolled full time or part time after October 1982 in a private, not-for-profit less-than-2-year institution; a private, for-profit less-than-2-year institution; or a public less-than-2-year institution.

Other enrollment
: Student enrolled in a postsecondary institution that did not fit into one of the other categories (e.g., a 4-year proprietary institution).

Undergraduate major (UGMAJOR)

Undergraduate majors were recorded for bachelor's degree recipients in this composite variable. Majors were reported by students and recorded by a 2-digit Classification of Instructional program (CIP) code. These codes were then aggregated into the categories shown here.

Agriculture/home economics

Business/marketing

Journalism/communications

Education

Math/computer science/engineering

Health

Sciences (e.g., biology, chemistry)

Social sciences (e.g., economics, psychology)

Art/music

Letters/languages/history

Other

Other Education Variables

College expectations in sixth grade (YB072A)

Yes, decided to go	Student expected while in sixth grade to attend college.
Planned not to go	Student expected while in sixth grade not to attend college.
Not sure	Student was not sure whether he or she would attend college.
Hadn't thought about it	Student had not thought about college while in the sixth grade.

Father's 1982 after-high-school aspirations for children (FY63A) and *mother's 1982 after-high-school aspirations for children (FY63B)*

These variables record the respondent's mother's and father's after-high-school aspirations for respondent at the time of the first follow-up survey in 1982. These are student-reported variables.

Go to college	Parent wants sophomore to go to college after high school.

Full-time job	Parent wants sophomore to work full time after high school.
Trade school	Parent wants sophomore to go to a trade school after high school.
Military service	Parent wants sophomore to go into the military after high school.

Grades in high school (HSGRADES)

This is primarily a student-reported variable combining data from the base-year and first follow-up surveys, but it also includes some data from the transcript surveys. The variable categories are described both as letter grades (e.g., mostly As) and as their numerical equivalents on a 100-point scale.

Mostly As (90–100)

Half As and Half Bs (85–89)

Mostly Bs (80–84)

Half Bs and half Cs (75–79)

Mostly Cs (70–74)

Half Cs and half Ds (65–69)

Mostly Ds (60–64)

High school diploma type (HSDIPLOM)

Regular diploma	Student received a high school diploma, and either graduated early or on time (June 1982).
Returned for diploma	Student stopped out at some point during high school or did not graduate on time, but returned to high school to finish their diploma or general equivalency diploma (GED).
Returned but no diploma	Student stopped out at some point during high school or did not graduate on time, returned to high school at a later time, but did not complete a diploma or GED.
Never returned	Student dropped out of high school and did not complete a diploma or GED at a later time.

Program in high school

> General
>
> Students reported that their high school program was neither vocational nor academic.

> Academic
>
> Students reported that their high school program was academic.

> Vocational
>
> Students reported that their high school program was vocational.

Repeated grade/held back (FY59)

> Never repeated
>
> Student did not report repeating a grade or being held back a term at some time between the first and ninth grades.

> Repeated grade
>
> Student reported repeating a grade or being held back a term at some time between the first and ninth grades.

Test score composite 1982 (FUTEST)

FUTEST in the Fourth Followup is a percentile composite based on the variable FUTEST from the First Followup in 1982. Originally, this variable was coded as a standard normal variable with a zero mean and a variance of 1, and was a composite score based on the average non-missing reading, vocabulary, and mathematics (part 1) test scores. The original standardized test score composite was converted to a percentile format by ranking students on an index that ranged from 1 to 100. Two versions of this variable were used in this report: as mean column values for groups defined in the rows (table 1.1); and as a row variable with the following format:

> Low quartile
>
> Students whose percentile rank ranged from 1 to 25 percent.

> Middle two quartiles
>
> Students whose percentile rank ranged from 26 to 75 percent.

> High quartile
>
> Students whose percentile rank ranged from 76 to 100 percent.

Demographic and Status Variables

Family income in 1980 (FAMINC)

Family income is based on sophomore- and parent-reported data from the base year survey. This variable was recoded from earlier surveys for inclusion in the HS&B Fourth Followup Data Analysis System file.

Less than $8,000

$8,000–$14,999

$15,000–$19,999

$20,000–$24,999

$25,000–$29,999

$30,000–$39,999

$40,000–$49,999

$50,000 or more

Father's occupation in 1980 (BB038)

Father's occupation is based on data reported by sophomores in the 1980 base year survey. Students were asked to describe their father's most recent job and to categorize his occupation into one of 16 standard occupational classifications. The job description and classifications were reviewed for consistency and recoded where obvious inconsistencies were apparent.

Clerical	Bank teller, bookkeeper, typist, secretary, mail carrier, ticket agent.
Craftsman	Baker, automobile mechanic, machinist, painter, plumber, telephone installer, carpenter.
Farmer, farm manager	
Homemaker only	
Laborer	Construction worker, car washer, sanitary worker, farm laborer
Manager, administrator	Sales manager, office manager, school administrator, buyer, restaurant manager, government official.
Military	Career officer, enlisted man in armed forces.
Operative	Meat cutter, assembler, machine operator, welder, taxicab, bus, or truck driver.

Professional	Accountant, artist, registered nurse, engineer, librarian, writer, social worker, actor, athlete, politician. Excludes school teachers.
Professional	Clergyman, dentist, physician, lawyer, scientist, college teacher.
Proprietor/owner	Small business owner, construction contractor, restaurant owner.
Protective services	Detective, police officer, security guard, sheriff, fire fighter.
Sales	Salesperson, advertising or insurance agent, real estate broker.
School teacher	Elementary or secondary.
Service	Barber, beautician, practical nurse, private household worker, janitor, waiter.
Technical	Draftsman, medical and dental technician, computer programmer.

Language spoken at home in 1982 (HOMELANG)

This is a composite variable created from student-reported data in the base-year language file. This file only contains data on students who reported that a non-English language was spoken in their home.

Single non-English language	A non-English language is the only language spoken in the home
Non-English language dominant	A non-English language is the predominant language used in the home, but English is also spoken.
Combination of languages	More than one language was reported as being spoken in the home with no single language being dominant.
English is the dominant language	Composite category that includes students who reported more than one language spoken in the home with English the predominant language, as well as students who did not report any other languages but English.

Mother worked before elementary school (BB037C), while in elementary school (BB037B), while in high school (BB037A)

Students were asked whether their mothers worked outside of the home at various stages of the students' lives. Each of these variables has the same set of row categories.

Did not work	Mother did not work outside of the home.
Part-time work	Mother worked part time outside the home.
Full-time work	Mother worked full time outside the home.

Occupational aspiration for age 30 in 1982 (FY77A)

Occupational aspirations are based on data reported by 1980 sophomores in the first follow-up survey in 1982. Respondents were asked to describe their job aspirations at age 30 and to categorize this occupation into one of 16 standard occupational classifications. The job description and classifications were reviewed for consistency and recoded where obvious inconsistencies were apparent.

Clerical	Bank teller, bookkeeper, typist, secretary, mail carrier, ticket agent.
Craftsman	Baker, automobile mechanic, machinist, painter, plumber, telephone installer, carpenter.
Farmer, farm manager	
Homemaker only	
Laborer	Construction worker, car washer, sanitary worker, farm laborer
Manager, administrator	Sales manager, office manager, school administrator, buyer, restaurant manager, government official.
Military	Career officer, enlisted man in armed forces.
Operative	Meat cutter, assembler, machine operator, welder, taxicab, bus, or truck driver.
Professional	Accountant, artist, registered nurse, engineer, librarian, writer, social worker, actor, athlete, politician. Excludes school teachers.

Professional	Clergyman, dentist, physician, lawyer, scientist, college teacher.
Proprietor/owner	Small business owner, construction contractor, restaurant owner.
Protective services	Detective, police officer, security guard, sheriff, fire fighter.
Sales	Salesperson, advertising or insurance agent, real estate broker.
School teacher	Elementary or secondary.
Service	Barber, beautician, practical nurse, private household worker, janitor, waiter.
Technical	Draftsman, medical and dental technician, computer programmer.

Parents' educational attainment in 1980 (PAREDUC)

PAREDUC is a composite variable that records the higher level of educational attainment for the respondent's father or mother. The variable is based on student-reported data on the base-year and first follow up surveys.

No high school diploma	Neither of the student's parents had completed a high school diploma as of 1980.
High school graduate	One or both of the student's parents had completed a high school diploma by 1980.
Vocational/technical	One or both of the student's parents had earned a vocational/technical degree, diploma, or certificate.
Some college	One or both of the student's parents had completed one or more years of college. One or both parents may have also completed a postsecondary degree less than a bachelor's degree other than a vocational-technical certificate.
Bachelor's degree	One or both of the student's parents had completed a bachelor's degree or bachelor's degree plus a fifth year certificate (such as a teaching credential).
Advanced degree	One or both of the student's parents had completed a master's degree, professional degree, or doctorate.

Political beliefs in 1980 (BB094)

Student-reported political beliefs in the base-year survey.

Popularity in 1982 (FY74A)

Very popular	Student believes self to be very popular with peers.
Somewhat popular	Student believes self to be somewhat popular with peers.
Not at all popular	Student believes self to be not at all popular with peers.

Race–ethnicity (RACE4)

This is a composite variable that draws upon information from the fourth follow-up and from earlier surveys. Two versions of this variable appear in the tables of this report, but the only difference between these variables is that one version distinguishes among Hispanics by their country of origin, while the other version has a single Hispanic category.

Native American/Alaska Native	A person having origins in any of the original peoples of North America and who maintains cultural identification through tribal affiliation or community recognition.
Asian/Pacific Islander	A person having origins in any of the Pacific Islander original peoples of the Far East, Southeast Asia, the Indian Subcontinent, or Pacific Islands. This includes people from China, Japan, Korea, the Philippine Islands, Samoa, India, and Vietnam.
Black, non-Hispanic	A person having origins in any of the black racial groups of Africa, except those of Hispanic origin.
White, non-Hispanic	A person having origins in any of the original peoples of the Europe, North Africa, or the Middle East (except those of Hispanic origin).
Hispanic	A person of Mexican, Puerto Rican, Cuban, Central or South American, or other Spanish culture or origin, regardless of race. The four Hispanic subgroups that are shown separately in some of the tables are Mexican, Puerto Rican, Cuban, and other.

Religious background (BB091)

Student reported religious background in the base-year survey.

Self-concept (FYCONCPT), Locus-of control (FYLOCUS), and Community orientation (FYCOMMUN)

These three variables are scalar measures of 1980 high school sophomores' self-concepts, sense of control over their lives, and attitudes about the importance of community, respectively. Each of these scale variables is a composite measure of a series of questions administered during the First Followup in 1982. These variables were originally coded as standard normal distribution with a zero mean and a variance of 1, but were converted to a percentile format for the Fourth Followup by ranking students' scores on an index that ranged from 1 to 100. These variables are reported only as mean column values for groups defined in the rows.

Sex (SEX)

    Male

    Female

Socioeconomic status (SES) composite 1980 (BYSES)

BYSES in the Fourth Followup is a percentile composite based on the variable BYSES from the 1980 base year file. Originally, this variable was coded as a standard normal variable with a zero mean and a variance of 1, and was a composite score based on the average non-missing values for father's occupation, father's education, mother's education, family income, and material possessions in the home. The original standardized test score composite was converted to a percentile format by ranking students on an index that ranged from 1 to 100. Two versions of this variable were used in this report: as mean column values for groups defined in the rows (table 1.1); and as a row variable with the following format:

Low quartile	Students whose percentile rank ranged from 1 to 25 percent.
Middle two quartiles	Students whose percentile rank ranged from 26 to 75 percent.
High quartile	Students whose percentile rank ranged from 76 to 100 percent.

Time watching TV (weekdays) in 1982 (FY61)

Student-reported number of hours of TV on weekdays in 1982.

Values cited as "important" by 1980 high school sophomores in 1992

Respondents were asked whether they valued the following (yes or no):

Providing their children with better opportunities than they had (VALUOPPR)

Money (VALUMONY)

Steady work (VALUSTED)

Strong friendships (VALUFRND)

Success in their work (VALUWORK)

Employment Variables

Real earnings in first year after terminating education (RELERNA1)

In order to facilitate comparisons of earnings across different levels of degree attainment and the year in which 1980 sophomores terminated their education, real earnings have been recorded for respondents both in relation to the timing of their highest degree attained and also in relation to their last enrollment in postsecondary education. Real earnings are reported in 1992 dollars, and nominal earnings were adjusted using the Consumer Price Index (CPI). Real earnings data are stored as continuous variables in the HS&B Fourth Followup Data Analysis System files.

Real earnings in third year after terminating education (RELERNA3)

See description of real earnings in first year after terminating education (RELERNA1) for explanation of this variable.

Earnings in 1991 (Y4301B9)

Earnings are stored as a continuous variable. Earnings were reported by respondents on an annual basis from 1983 through 1991.

Employment status February 1992 (EMST9202)
The HS&B Data Analysis System files contain a monthly employment status variable for each respondent from January 1986 through June 1992, although missing data are a problem for the months after February 1992. Each monthly employment status variable includes four categories.

Working   Employed in the month specified either full time or part time.

Unemployed, receiving benefits	Unemployed in the month specified and receiving unemployment benefits.
Unemployed, not receiving benefits	Unemployed in the month specified, but not receiving any unemployment benefits.
Out of the labor force	Not employed for pay outside of the home. This category also includes discouraged workers who are not looking for work.

Industry of Employment in 1992 (Y4303CA)

Agriculture	Includes also forestry and fisheries (private only).
Mining	
Construction	Examples include building trades such as carpenters and electricians.
Manufacturing–durable goods	
Manufacturing–non-durable goods	
Public utilities	Examples include transportation, communications, and organizations like the U.S. Postal Service, Federal Express, and travel agents.
Wholesale trade	
Retail trade	
Finance	Also includes insurance and real estate.
Business and repair services	Examples include industries such as auto repair, business agents, public relations, advertising, and photo developing.
Personal services	Examples include cleaners, beauty shops, funeral homes, hotels and restaurants, and domestics.
Recreation services	Examples include entertainment and recreation, amusement parks, bowling alleys, and theaters.
Professional services	Examples include public and private hospitals, schools, social services, health practitioners such as doctors, dentists, nurses, and chiropractors.

Public administration

Occupation of employment in 1992 (Y4303FA)

The occupation variable contains 29 categories, not all of which are shown in the tables of this report. These 29 categories can be collapsed to the 16 standard Dictionary of Occupational Titles (DOT) categories that were used to record father's, mother's, and respondent's occupation in earlier surveys. The full 29 categories are shown here.

Clerical, secretarial	Secretary, typist, file clerk, receptionist, word processor.
Clerical, financial	Bookkeeper, bank teller.
Clerical, other	Ticket agent, mail carrier, meter reader, shipping and receiving, telephone operator, library clerk, office machine operator, messenger, dispatcher.
Craftsperson	Baker, auto mechanic, machinist, plumber, house painter, carpenter, brick mason, telephone installer, other unspecified mechanics, tile setter, carpet installer, roofer.
Farmer/farm manager	
Homemaker	No other outside job.
Laborer	Construction worker, car washer, sanitary worker, farm laborer, machine cleaner, stock handler, bagger, loader, stevedore, tradesperson's helper, gas station attendant, handyperson.
Manager/administrator–sales/purchasing	Sales manager, buyer.
Manager/administrator–government	Local, state, or federal.
Manager/administrator–retail, hospitality	Store, restaurant, hotel, etc.
Manager/administrator–manufacturing, construction	Line supervisor, etc.
Manager/administrator–other	

Skilled operative	Truck driver, assembler, machine operator, welder, inspector, bus driver, forklift operator, train engineer, cab driver, chauffeur, sewing machine operator, printing press operator.
Professional–arts/ entertainment/media	Actor, artist, writer, athlete, designer, editor, disc jockey, publicist, photographer.
Professional–medical	Nurse, social worker. Excludes physicians.
Professional–engineer	
Professional–physician	
Professional–legal	
Professional–other	Clergyman, scientist, college professor, other postsecondary teacher, psychologist, accountant.
Proprietor/owner–retail/ hospitality	Store, restaurant, hotel, motel.
Proprietor/owner–manufacturing and construction	Construction contractor.
Proprietor/owner–other	
Protective services	Detective, police, fire fighter, security guard, crossing guard, FBI agent.
Sales	Salesperson, advertising or insurance agent, real estate broker, counter held, cashier.
School teacher	Elementary or secondary.
Service	Barber, beautician, janitor, waitperson, practical nurse, nurse's aide, maid, orderly, cook, kitchen help, exterminator, flight attendant.
Technical–computer related	Programmer, computer technician, systems analyst.
Technical–noncomputer related	Draftsperson, medical/dental technician.

Other Variables

Activities in week prior to survey in June 1992 (Y4103A–Y4103K)

Students were asked to describe their major activities in the week prior to being surveyed in June 1992.

Working

Looking for work

On temporary layoff

Taking vocational/technical courses

Taking undergraduate/academic courses

Taking graduate/professional courses

In apprenticeship or training program

On active duty in the armed forces

Keeping house

Taking a break

Other

Community lived in February 1982 (FY100)

This variable is a student-reported measure of the degree of urbanization of the community in which the student lived in February 1982.

Rural/farm	A rural or farming community.
Small city	A small city or town of fewer than 50,000 people that is not a suburb of a larger place.
Medium city	A city of between 50,000 and 100,000 residents.
Suburb, medium city	A suburb of a medium-sized city.
Large city	A city of 100,000 to 500,000 people.

Suburb, large city	A suburb of a large city.
Huge city	A city with more than 500,000 people.
Suburb, huge city	A suburb of a huge city.
Military base	A military base or station.

Marital Status in June 1992 (MARST92)

Married	Respondent was married in June 1992.
Separated	Respondent was separated from spouse in June 1992.
Divorced	Respondent had been married but was divorced in June 1992.
Widowed	Respondent had been married but the spouse died sometime before June 1992.
Never married	Respondent had never been married.
Living in a marriage-like relationship	Respondent reported living with a partner but not being married.

Marital and parental status in 1992 (FMFRM92)

Married, no children

Married, with children

Divorced/separated/widowed, no children

Never married, no children

Never married, with children

Living together, no children

Living together, with children

Number of marriages (TMSMAR92)

Stored as a continuous variable on the HS&B Fourth Followup Data Analysis System files.

Urbanicity of high school area (HSURBAN)

This variable classifies the community where the respondent's high school was located according to the CIC urbanization code.

Urban	Urban or central city.
Suburban	Suburban, in SMSA but not in central city.
Rural	Rural, or not in SMSA

Volunteer activities in 1992 (Y4502A–Y4502J)

The 1980 high school sophomores were asked to describe any volunteer activities in which they had been engaged in the year prior to being surveyed.

Any volunteer groups or organizations (yes/no)

Youth organizations such as little league coach, scout leader, etc.

Union, farm, trade, or professional associations

Political clubs or organizations

Organized volunteer work such as in a hospital

Sports teams or clubs

Educational organizations such as PTA or academic group

Service clubs such as Rotary, Chamber of Commerce, Veterans, Lions, Kiwanis, Elks, etc.

Other volunteer groups

Voting indicators

Registered in 1986 (TY56)

Registered in 1992 (Y4503)

Voted in presidential election in 1984 (TY58)

Voted in non-presidential local, state or national elections in 1988 (Y4504)

Voted in presidential election in 1988 (Y4505)

Appendix B: Technical Notes

Appendix B
Technical Notes

The High School and Beyond Fourth Followup

The High School and Beyond (HS&B) survey began in the spring of 1980 with the collection of base year questionnaire and test data on over 58,000 high school seniors and sophomores. The first followup survey was conducted in the spring of 1982, the second followup in the spring of 1984, the third followup in the spring of 1986, and the fourth followup in the spring of 1992.

The HS&B Fourth Followup Survey is the fifth wave of the longitudinal study, but unlike previous rounds, the fourth followup focused exclusively on a sophomore class. The Fourth Followup included two components: a respondent survey with sample of 14,825 members of the 1980 sophomore cohort, and a transcript study based on the 9,064 sophomore cohort members who reported postsecondary attendance. The goals of the fourth followup were to obtain information on issues of access to and choice of undergraduate and graduate educational institutions, persistence in attaining educational goals and progress through the curriculum, rates of degree attainment and of other educational outcomes, and labor market outcomes in relation to educational attainment and labor market experiences.

Sample design. In the base year, students were selected using a two-stage, stratified probability sample design with schools as the first-stage units and students within schools as the second-stage units.[1] The total number of schools selected for the sample was 1,122, from a frame of 24,725 schools with grades 10 or 12 or both. Within each stratum schools were selected with probabilities proportional to the estimated enrollment in their 10th and 12th grades. Within each school, 36 seniors and 36 sophomores were randomly selected. In those schools with fewer than 36 seniors or 36 sophomores, all eligible students were drawn in the sample.

The first follow-up sophomore and senior cohort samples were based on the HS&B base year samples, retaining the essential features of a stratified multi-stage design (for further details see Tourangeau, et al., 1983).[2] Subsequent to the first followup survey, high school transcripts were sought for a probability subsample of nearly 18,500 members of the 1980 sophomore cohort. The subsampling plan for the Transcript Study emphasized the retention of members of subgroups of special relevance for education policy analysis. Compared to the base year and first followup surveys, the Transcript Study sample design further increased the overrepresentation of racial and ethnic minorities (especially those with above average HS&B achievement test scores), students who attended private high schools, school dropouts, transfers and early

---

[1]For further details on the base year sample design see Frankel, M.; Kohnke, L.; Buonanno, D.; and Tourangeau, R. (1981), High School and Beyond Sample Design Report. Chicago: National Opinion Research Center.

[2]Tourangeau, R.; McWilliams, H.; Jones, C.; Frankel, M.; and O'Brien, F. (1983), *High School and Beyond First Follow-Up (1982) Sample Design Report*. Chicago: National Opinion Research Center.

graduates, and students whose parents participated in the base year Parent's Survey on financing postsecondary education.

The samples for the second and third followup surveys of the 1980 sophomore cohort were based upon the transcript study design. A total of 14,825 cases were selected from among the 18,500 retained for the transcript study. As was the case for the transcript sample, the sophomore cohort second and third follow-up samples included disproportionate numbers of sample members from policy-relevant subpopulations (e.g., racial and ethnic minorities, students from private high schools, high school dropouts, students who planned to pursue some type of postsecondary schooling, and so on).[3] The members of the senior cohort selected into the second follow-up sample consisted exactly of those selected into the first follow-up sample. The third followup was the last one conducted for the senior cohort.

The fourth followup is composed solely of members from the sophomore cohort. The members of the sophomore cohort selected into the fourth follow-up sample consisted exactly of those selected into the second and third follow-up sample. For any student who ever enrolled in postsecondary education, complete transcript information was requested from the institutions indicated by the student.

Sample weights. The general purpose of weighting is to compensate for the unequal probability of selection into the sample, and to adjust for respondent nonresponse to the survey. The weights are based on the inverse of the selection probabilities at each stage of the sample selection process and on nonresponse adjustment factors computed within weighting cells. The fourth followup had two major components, the collection of survey data and the collection of postsecondary transcript data. Nonresponse occurred during both of these data collection phases. Weights were computed to account for nonresponse during either phase. For the survey data, two weights were computed. The first weight (FU4WT) was computed for all fourth follow-up respondents. The second weight (PANEL5WT) was computed for all fourth follow-up respondents who also participated in the base year and first, second and third followup surveys. For more information about the design and implementation of the survey weights, see the High School and Beyond Fourth Followup Methodology Report.[4]

Accuracy of Estimates

The estimates in this report are derived from samples and are subject to two broad classes of error—sampling and nonsampling error. Sampling errors occur because the data are collected from a sample of a population rather than from the entire population. Estimates based on a sample will differ somewhat from the values that would have been obtained from a universe survey using the same instruments, instructions, and procedures. Nonsampling errors come from

---

[3]See Tables 2.4-1 through 2.4-4 of C. Jones and B. D. Spencer (1985), *High School and Beyond Second Follow-Up (1984) Sample Design Report.* Chicago: National Opinion Research Center.

[4]Zahs, Pedlow, Morrissey, Marnell, and Nichols, *The High School and Beyond Fourth Follow-Up Methodology Report* (U.S. Department of Education, National Center for Education Statistics, Postsecondary Longitudinal Studies Branch, 1994), Section 3.

a variety of sources and affect universe surveys as well as sample surveys. Examples of sources of nonsampling error include design, reporting, and processing errors and errors due to nonresponse. The effects of nonsampling errors are more difficult to evaluate than those that result from sampling variability. As much as possible, procedures are built into surveys in order to minimize nonsampling errors.

The standard error is a measure of the variability due to sampling when estimating a parameter. It indicates how much variance there is in the population of possible estimates of a parameter for a given sample size. Standard errors can be used as a measure of the precision expected from a particular sample. The probability that a complete census would differ from the sample by less than the standard error is about 68 out of 100. The chances that the difference would be less than 1.65 times the standard error are about 90 out of 100; that the difference would be less than 1.96 times the standard error, about 95 out of 100. Selected standard errors are presented in table B.1, and standard errors for the essay tables are presented in Appendix C.

Data Analysis System

The estimates presented in this report were produced using the NCES Data Analysis System (DAS) for the HS&B Fourth Followup. The DAS software makes it possible for users to specify and generate their own tables from the HS&B data. With the DAS, users can recreate or expand upon the tables presented in this report. In addition to the table estimates, the DAS calculates appropriate standard errors and weighted sample sizes for the estimates.[5] For example, table B.1 presents the standard errors that correspond to table 1.1 in the table compendium. If the number of valid cases is too small to produce an estimate, the DAS prints the message "low-N" instead of the estimate (converted to a "—" in the Compendium tables).

In addition to the tables, the DAS will also produce a correlation matrix of selected variables that can be used in linear regression models, and the design effects (DEFT) for all the parameter estimates in the correlation matrix. Since statistical procedures generally compute regression coefficients based on simple random sample assumptions, the standard errors must be adjusted with the design effects to take into account the complex sampling procedures used in the HS&B surveys.

---

[5]The HSB sample is not a simple random sample, and techniques for estimating standard errors that are appropriate for simple random samples will not produce accurate standard errors for these data. The DAS takes into account the complex sampling procedures and calculates standard errors that are appropriate for of the variable

For more information about the 1992 HS&B Fourth Followup DAS, contact:
Aurora D'Amico
NCES Longitudinal Studies Branch
555 New Jersey Ave., N.W.
Washington, D.C., 20208-5652
(202) 219-1365
Internet address: ADAMICO@INET.ED.GOV

Methodology and Statistical Procedures

The comparisons in the text have all been tested for statistical significance to ensure that the differences are larger than those that might be expected due to sampling variation. Three types of comparisons have been made in the text.

Differences in two estimated percentages. The Student's t statistic was used to test the likelihood that the differences between two percentages were larger than would be expected due to sampling error. The Student's t values can be computed for comparisons using the estimates in these tables with the following formula:

$$t = \frac{P_1 - P_2}{\sqrt{se_{1^2} + se_{2^2}}}$$

where P_1 and P_2 are the estimates to be compared and se_1 and se_2 are their corresponding standard errors. This formula is only valid for independent estimates. When estimates are not independent (for example, when comparing the percentages within a percent distribution—in this report, within a row in a table), a covariance term was added to the denominator of the t-test formula.

There are hazards in reporting statistical tests for each comparison. First, large t-values may appear to merit special attention. However, the magnitude of the t-statistic is related not only to the observed differences in means or percentages, but also to the number of students in the categories that are being compared. A small difference compared across a large number of students will produce a large t-statistic.

Second, as the number of comparisons on the same set of data increases, the likelihood that the t value for at least one of the comparisons will exceed 1.96 simply due to sampling error increases. For a single comparison, there is a 5 percent chance that the t value will exceed 1.96 due to sampling error. For five tests, the risk of getting at least one t value that high increases to 23 percent, and for 20 comparisons, it increases to 64 percent.

One way to compensate for this danger when making multiple comparisons is to adjust the critical value that the t-statistic must equal or exceed to take into account the number of comparisons being made. This is done using a Bonferroni adjustment to control for the number of possible comparisons—the family of comparisons—between the categories of the variable being tested. Family size, k, is calculated as follows: k = [j * (j - 1)]/2, where j is equal to the number of categories in the variable. In a 5-category variable such as parent's education, k would be equal to [(5)(5-1)]/2, or 10. The family size is then used to adjust the probability that one would incorrectly conclude that two estimates were different because of sampling error. Differences between two estimates were only reported when $p \leq 0.05/k$, or in the case of parents' education, when $p \leq 0.005$ (that is, 0.05/10). In order to conclude that two estimates were different in this case, the critical value that the t-statistic had to equal or exceed was 2.81, which was obtained from a table of t statistics for a two-tailed test.

Trends. In several instances, pair-wise comparisons proved too cumbersome. For example, one would like to say something about the general relationship between the percentage of 1980 high school sophomores with a postsecondary degree and their parents' level of educational attainment. In many cases, not all of the ten possible comparisons are statistically significant, even though the data appear to suggest clear trends. In such cases, a weighted least squares regression formula was used to test whether the upward trend between parents' attainment and the percentage of sophomores with a postsecondary degree was significant, even if all of the pair-wise comparisons were not.

This regression test for linearity was done in this analysis using the data manipulation and regression capabilities of the Microsoft EXCEL spreadsheet program. The input data for the regressions were the estimates and standard errors in the output tables created by the Data Analysis System. All of the variables included in the regression equations were transformed by dividing them by the standard error of the relevant proportion. An intercept variable was also created by diving a column of 1s by the standard error of the corresponding proportion. The new dependent variable was then regressed on the new independent variable and the intercept variable. The statistical significance of beta for the independent variable was then evaluated in relation $p \leq 0.05$, or $t \geq 1.96$. One important limitation of this test is that it can only be used to assess trends across ordered variables or variable categories.

Differences in distributions. The third type of test used in this report is the chi-square test, which was used to assess whether one distribution was different from another. For example, one would like to evaluate the highest level of educational attainment in 1992 of the 1980 sophomores in relation to their educational expectations in 1982. Even with the advanced degree categories (master's, professional, and doctorate) collapsed into a single category, there are five levels of postsecondary attainment (none, vocational certificate, associate degree, bachelor degree, and advanced degree), and five levels of postsecondary expectations, which implies 120 (i.e., 5!) pair-wise comparisons. In this instance, the chi-square test enables one to evaluate whether for each level of expectations the attainment distributions are different with a single test.

Once the chi-square value is calculated, it is adjusted by the cell-specific design effects (DEFT)—rather than the average DEFT for the whole sample—to take into account the complex sample design. These effects were estimated using a Microsoft EXCEL spreadsheet model, which is based on work by Rao and Thomas.[6] In general, this adjustment reduces the value of the chi-square (because complex samples are not as efficient as simple random samples of equivalent

---

[6]J.N.K. Rao and D.R. Thomas, "Chi-Squared Tests for Contingency Tables," in Skinner, Holt, and Smith, *Analysis of Complex Surveys* (New York: Wiley and Sons, 1989), chapter 4.

size). This value is then evaluated in relation to a critical value that is obtained from a table for a test with n degrees of freedom and a specified signficance level. In this case, the signficance level was set at $p \leq 0.05$. The degrees of freedom were calculated as the number of row categories minus 1 times the number of column categories minus 1.

Table B.1—Standard errors for Table 1.1: Average percentile rank of 1980 high school sophomores in specialized composite scales, by selected characteristics

Student characteristics	Socio-economic status (1980)	Test scores (1982)	Self-concept (1982)	Locus of control (1982)	Community orientation (1982)
Total	0.50	0.49	0.40	0.41	0.42
Sex					
Male	0.60	0.62	0.54	0.59	0.58
Female	0.62	0.59	0.51	0.51	0.53
Race–ethnicity					
Native American/Alaska Native	2.07	2.75	2.59	3.49	2.91
Asian/Pacific Islander	2.45	2.41	1.93	1.50	1.71
Black	1.04	0.94	1.05	1.26	1.03
White	0.52	0.49	0.44	0.44	0.42
Hispanic-Mexican	1.72	1.59	1.67	1.73	1.47
Hispanic-Cuban	3.78	4.13	2.77	2.89	3.03
Hispanic-Puerto Rican	2.56	2.42	3.39	2.75	2.47
Hispanic-other	2.11	1.82	2.36	2.63	2.25
Family income in 1980					
Less than $8,000	1.25	1.56	1.59	1.57	1.55
$8,000–$14,999	0.89	1.14	0.93	0.97	0.95
$15,000–$19,999	0.88	1.05	0.99	0.96	0.99
$20,000–$24,999	0.92	1.05	0.93	1.05	0.95
$25,000–$29,999	0.83	0.97	0.91	0.87	0.93
$30,000–$39,999	0.79	0.93	0.90	0.84	0.99
$40,000–$49,999	1.07	1.29	1.15	1.12	1.24
$50,000 or more	0.95	1.27	1.13	1.05	1.11
Father's occupation in 1980					
Technical	1.00	1.83	1.69	1.68	1.76
Clerical	1.42	2.33	2.23	2.28	2.34
Craftsman	0.66	0.94	0.96	0.97	0.98
Farmer	1.22	1.79	1.72	1.78	1.66
Laborer	0.83	1.13	1.11	1.19	1.14
Manager	0.66	1.03	1.05	0.97	1.15
Military	2.03	2.77	2.94	3.00	2.59
Operative	0.73	1.00	1.07	1.01	1.06
Professional	0.93	1.58	1.48	1.41	1.53
Professional/doctor	0.66	1.43	1.71	1.65	1.82
Proprietor/owner	0.95	1.40	1.37	1.26	1.40
Protective service	1.52	2.10	1.87	2.07	2.09
Sales	1.01	1.51	1.68	1.54	1.69
School teacher	1.34	3.24	2.99	2.78	3.21
Service	2.01	2.81	2.85	2.62	2.34
Program in high school					
General	0.72	0.68	0.74	0.78	0.81
Academic	0.65	0.58	0.51	0.47	0.53
Vocational	0.64	0.59	0.67	0.74	0.66
Urbanicity of high school area					
Urban	1.19	1.35	0.88	1.06	0.94
Suburb	0.76	0.77	0.57	0.58	0.60
Rural	0.87	0.76	0.70	0.72	0.77

Table B.1—Standard errors for Table 1.1: Average percentile rank of 1980 high school sophomores in specialized composite scales, by selected characteristics— Continued

Student characteristics	Socio-economic status (1980)	Test scores (1982)	Self-concept (1982)	Locus of control (1982)	Community orientation (1982)
Community lived in Feb 1982					
Rural/farm	0.78	0.88	0.75	0.76	0.74
Small city	0.79	0.75	0.65	0.60	0.60
Medium city	1.03	1.11	0.83	0.89	0.88
Burb medium city	1.39	1.67	1.10	1.21	1.16
Large city	1.53	1.51	1.07	1.16	1.09
Burb large city	1.44	1.44	1.26	1.24	1.28
Huge city	2.08	2.39	1.57	1.79	1.63
Burb huge city	1.91	2.12	1.60	1.77	1.61
Military base	3.37	3.49	2.94	3.54	3.92
Religious background in 1980					
Baptist	0.87	0.98	0.88	0.94	0.85
Methodist	1.28	1.25	1.09	1.16	1.30
Lutheran	1.27	1.41	1.33	1.42	1.36
Presbyterian	1.82	1.79	1.80	1.82	1.83
Episcopalian	2.59	2.63	2.30	2.26	2.36
Other protestant	1.92	1.85	1.94	1.82	1.89
Catholic	0.72	0.65	0.60	0.60	0.61
Other Christian	1.42	1.53	1.55	1.49	1.53
Jewish	3.04	2.47	3.21	3.12	3.35
Other religion	1.66	1.60	1.55	1.68	1.78
None	1.61	1.77	1.50	1.52	1.64
Political beliefs in 1980					
Conservative	1.35	1.53	1.36	1.23	1.33
Moderate	0.72	0.70	0.67	0.65	0.70
Liberal	1.08	1.08	1.02	1.05	0.98
Radical	1.72	1.94	1.63	1.75	1.81
None	1.24	1.20	1.21	1.31	1.22
Grades in high school					
Mostly A 90–100	1.61	1.32	1.57	1.31	1.56
Half A/B 85–89	0.95	0.92	0.88	0.79	0.90
Mostly B 80–84	0.82	0.77	0.71	0.68	0.71
Half B/C 75–79	0.73	0.67	0.66	0.63	0.69
Mostly C 70–74	0.78	0.74	0.77	0.76	0.79
Half C/D 65–69	1.09	0.91	1.15	1.26	1.26
Mostly D 60–64	2.43	1.59	2.57	3.52	2.87
Parents educational attainment by 1980					
High school	0.44	0.59	0.60	0.62	0.64
Vocational/technical	0.61	0.87	0.82	0.81	0.92
Some college	0.57	0.81	0.70	0.71	0.76
Bachelor's degree	0.69	1.11	1.12	1.04	1.11
Advanced degree	0.76	1.44	1.61	1.38	1.73

SOURCE: National Center for Education Statistics, High School & Beyond: 1980 Sophomore Cohort, 1980–1992.

Appendix C: Essay Standard Error Tables

Standard errors for Table 1
Percentage of 1980 high school sophomores by highest degree attained through 1992, by postsecondary expectations in 1982

Student characteristics	Highest degree through 1992							
	Less than high school graduate	High school	Certi-ficate	Assoc-iate's	Bachelor's	Master's	Profes-sional	Doctorate
Total	0.34	0.70	0.43	0.31	0.55	0.20	0.10	0.05
Postsecondary expectations in 1982								
None	1.01	1.25	0.72	0.42	0.21	0.10	0.00	0.07
Vocational-technical	0.56	1.28	1.06	0.82	0.46	0.07	0.00	0.00
Less than four-year degree	0.35	1.54	1.12	1.07	1.00	0.31	0.12	0.00
College degree	0.22	1.28	0.61	0.58	1.27	0.55	0.22	0.04
Advanced degree	0.26	1.41	0.68	0.63	1.46	0.77	0.50	0.26

SOURCE: National Center for Education Statistics, High School & Beyond: Sophomore Cohort 1980–1992

Standard errors for Table 2
Percentage of 1980 high school sophomores by highest degree attained through 1992, by immediate versus delayed entry

Entry status	Highest degree through 1992				
	High school	Certi-ficate	Assoc-iate's	Bachelor's	Advanced degree
Immediate entrants	0.84	0.53	0.56	0.89	0.47
Delayed entrants	1.41	1.24	0.89	0.76	0.26

SOURCE: National Center for Education Statistics, High School & Beyond: Sophomore Cohort 1980–1992

Standard errors for Table 3
Percentage of 1980 high school sophomores by highest degree attained through 1992, by postsecondary expectations in 1982 among immediate versus delayed entrants

Postsecondary expectations in 1982	Highest degree through 1992				
	High school	Certificate	Associate's	Bachelor's	Advanced degree
Immediate entrants					
None	5.18	4.78	3.63	2.46	0.00
Vocational-technical	2.48	2.28	2.04	1.21	0.27
Less than four-year degree	1.96	1.41	1.71	1.59	0.59
College degree	1.24	0.62	0.67	1.41	0.74
Advanced degree	1.36	0.56	0.7	1.55	1.05
Delayed entrants					
None	2.68	2.37	1.80	0.86	0.52
Vocational-technical	2.62	2.33	1.75	0.88	0.00
Less than four-year degree	3.08	2.58	0.90	2.13	0.49
College degree	3.49	2.53	2.01	2.59	0.79
Advanced degree	4.48	3.47	2.25	3.44	1.70

SOURCE: National Center for Education Statistics, High School & Beyond: Sophomore Cohort 1980–1992

Standard errors for Table 4
Percentage of 1980 high school sophomores by highest degree attained through 1992, by timing and intensity of initial postsecondary enrollment

Type of start in postsecondary education	Less than high school graduate	High school	Certi- ficate	Assoc- iate's	Bachelor's	Master's	Profes- sional	Doctorate
				Highest degree through 1992				
Total	0.34	0.70	0.43	0.31	0.55	0.20	0.10	0.05
4-year institution								
Full-time fall 1982	0.03	0.95	0.44	0.52	1.10	0.65	0.37	0.17
Part-time fall 1982	0.00	4.57	2.75	2.78	4.27	1.76	0.09	0.38
Delayed entry	0.23	2.92	1.45	1.67	2.21	1.10	0.31	0.33
2-year institution								
Full-time fall 1982	0.19	1.69	1.20	1.49	1.50	0.53	0.15	0.00
Part-time fall 1982	1.05	2.89	1.90	1.53	2.19	0.50	0.48	0.01
Delayed entry	0.42	1.92	1.52	1.27	0.90	0.16	0.00	0.00
Other institution								
Fall 1982	0.13	2.07	2.38	2.14	1.76	0.61	0.32	0.00
Delayed entry	0.55	2.53	2.75	1.85	0.89	0.07	0.07	0.00
Other enrollment	0.00	0.00	2.79	1.83	1.87	0.72	0.28	0.80
No enrollment	0.95	0.95	0.00	0.00	0.00	0.00	0.00	0.00

SOURCE: National Center for Education Statistics, High School & Beyond: Sophomore Cohort 1980–1992

Standard errors for Table 5
Average length of initial delay (in months) among 1980 high school sophomores who delayed entry into postsecondary education, by highest degree attained through 1992 and type of institution

Type of institution	Average length of delay (months)	Average length of delay in months by highest degree through 1992				
		High school	Certi-ficate	Assoc-iate's	Bachelor's	Advanced degree
Total	0.38	0.68	1.22	0.85	0.18	0.31
4-year	1.46	2.23	5.14	4.99	1.55	—
2-year public	1.13	1.50	2.87	2.43	2.27	—

—Sample size is too small for a reliable estimate.

SOURCE: National Center for Education Statistics, High School & Beyond: Sophomore Cohort 1980–1992

Standard errors for Table 6
Average length of initial delay before entering postsecondary education (in months) among 1980 high school sophomores, by highest degree attained through 1992 and postsecondary expectations

Postsecondary expectations (1982)	Average length of delay (months)	Average length of delay in months by highest degree through 1992				
		High school	Certi-ficate	Assoc-iate's	Bachelor's	Advanced degree
Total	0.38	0.68	1.22	0.85	0.18	0.31
None	1.66	2.24	3.15	4.67	—	—
Vocational-technical	1.01	1.44	1.98	1.80	1.89	—
Less than four-year degree	0.72	1.33	1.76	0.84	0.61	1.36
College degree	0.47	1.12	2.71	1.82	0.15	0.44
Advanced degree	0.33	1.05	1.08	1.83	0.26	0.36

—Sample size is too small for a reliable estimate.

SOURCE: National Center for Education Statistics, High School & Beyond: Sophomore Cohort 1980–1992

Standard errors for Table 7
Average length of initial delay before entering postsecondary education (in months) among 1980 high school sophomores, by highest degree attained through 1992, socioeconomic status quartile, and test score quartile

Student characteristic	Average length of delay (months)	Average length of delay in months by highest degree through 1992				
		High school	Certi-ficate	Assoc-iate's	Bachelor's	Advanced degree
Total	0.38	0.68	1.22	0.85	0.18	0.31
Socioeconomic status						
Low quartile	1.13	1.60	2.69	2.46	1.10	—
Middle two quartiles	0.49	0.94	1.29	0.97	0.26	0.38
High quartile	0.36	0.96	2.01	1.28	0.20	0.39
Test score composite (1982)						
Low quartile	1.44	1.79	3.07	2.72	1.91	—
Middle two quartiles	0.49	0.82	1.43	0.96	0.34	0.60
High quartile	0.33	1.14	2.26	1.02	0.18	0.19

—Sample size is too small for a reliable estimate.

SOURCE: National Center for Education Statistics, High School & Beyond: Sophomore Cohort 1980–1992

Standard errors for Table 8
Average number of months between first enrollment and attainment of degrees, by type of degree, postsecondary expectations, and timing and intensity of initial postsecondary enrollment

Postsecondary education characteristics	Certi- ficate	Assoc- iate's	Bachelor's
Total	1.07	0.89	0.44
Postsecondary expectations			
None	1.83	2.98	—
Vocational-technical	1.37	1.50	3.93
Less than 4-year degree	3.05	1.50	1.54
College degree	2.61	1.75	0.63
Advanced degree	3.23	2.50	0.55
Type of start in postsecondary education			
4-year institution			
Full-time fall 1982	2.77	2.25	0.43
Part-time fall 1982	—	—	4.28
Delayed entry	5.39	5.75	1.74
2-year institution			
Full-time fall 1982	3.54	1.21	1.51
Part-time fall 1982	4.82	4.51	3.55
Delayed entry	3.46	2.90	3.78
Other institution			
Fall 1982	1.75	2.16	2.18
Delayed entry	1.52	2.94	—

—Sample size is too small for a reliable estimate.

SOURCE: National Center for Education Statistics, High School & Beyond: Sophomore Cohort 1980–1992

Standard errors for Table 9
Average number of postsecondary institutions attended
by highest degree attained through 1992, by timing and
intensity of initial postsecondary enrollment

Type of start in postsecondary education	Certi-ficate	Assoc-iate's	Bachelor's
Total	0.03	0.03	0.02
4-year institution			
Full-time fall 1982	0.08	0.09	0.02
Part-time fall 1982	—	—	0.22
Delayed entry	0.15	0.15	0.07
2-year institution			
Full-time fall 1982	0.07	0.04	0.06
Part-time fall 1982	0.12	0.12	0.14
Delayed entry	0.11	0.09	0.13
Other institution			
Fall 1982	0.04	0.06	0.12
Delayed entry	0.04	0.08	—

—Sample size is too small for a reliable estimate.

SOURCE: National Center for Education Statistics, High School & Beyond: Sophomore Cohort 1980–1992